THE WILDLIFE
POCKET COMPANION

Edited by Malcolm Tait
and Olive Tayler

PAVILION

A Think Book for Pavilion Books

This edition published by Pavilion Books in 2008
First published in the United Kingdom in 2004 by Robson Books
10 Southcombe Street, London W14 0RA

Imprints of Anova Books Company Ltd

Text and design © Think Publishing 2004
The moral rights of the authors have been asserted

Edited by Malcolm Tait and Olive Tayler
The Companion team: Vicky Bamforth, Sarah Bove, James Collins,
Harry Glass, Rhiannon Guy, Annabel Holmes, Emma Jones
and Lou Millward Tait

Think Publishing
The Pall Mall Deposit
124–128 Barlby Road, London W10 6BL
www.thinkpublishing.co.uk

ISBN 978-1-862058-25-5

2 4 6 8 10 9 7 5 3 1

Printed and bound by Millenium International Printing, China

The publishers and authors have made every effort to ensure the
accuracy and currency of the information in *The Wildlife Pocket
Companion*. Similarly, every effort has been made to contact copyright
holders. We apologise for any unintentional errors or omissions.
The publisher and authors disclaim any liability, loss, injury or
damage incurred as a consequence, directly or indirectly, of the
use and application of the contents of this book.

www.anovabooks.com

THE POCKET COMPANION SERIES:
COLLECT THEM ALL

The Birdwatcher's Pocket Companion
by Malcolm Tait and Olive Tayler
ISBN 978-1-862057-97-5

The Cook's Pocket Companion
by Jo Swinnerton ISBN 978-1-862057-90-6

The Fishing Pocket Companion
by Lesley Crawford ISBN 978-1-862057-92-0

The London Pocket Companion
by Jo Swinnerton ISBN 978-1-862057-94-4

The Sailing Pocket Companion
by Miles Kendall ISBN 978-1-862057-96-8

The Traveller's Pocket Companion
by Georgina Newbery and Rhiannon Guy
ISBN 978-1-862057-91-3

The Walker's Pocket Companion
by Malcolm Tait ISBN 978-1-862057-93-7

The Golfer's Pocket Companion
by Chris Martin ISBN 978-1-862058-23-1

The Literary Pocket Companion
by Emma Jones ISBN 978-1-862058-24-8

The History of Britain Pocket Companion
by Jo Swinnerton ISBN 978-1-862058-22-4

The Gardener's Pocket Companion
by Vicky Bamforth ISBN 978-1-862057-95-1

INTRODUCTION

If you think you're buying a worthy reference book,
think again. But if you're looking for an original and
humorous snapshot of the natural world, look no
further. *The Wildlife Companion* opens up vistas that
will amuse and inform the most learned experts on
nature and conservation.

Yet the secret of this miscellany is its alternative take
on wildlife, which is certain to have a broad appeal.
Even those who would normally shun the animal and
plant kingdoms cannot fail to be captivated by the wry
observations, charming descriptions and torrent of
fascinating nature 'trivia'.

This encyclopaedic material is not just natural fodder
for the pub quiz night, it will nourish the minds of anyone
curious and hungry for knowledge, young and old. The
information may have a greater resonance for devotees of
the country walk, connoisseurs of safaris and expeditions
to the outback. But this canter through the undergrowth
and byways of our environment cannot fail to raise a
smile and strengthen respect for the living world.

This guide will teach you to mind your Jills and Kittens,
Hoglets and Scats. It will introduce you to a Cawdy
Mawdy, a Mouldiwarp, Hornywink, Leopard's bane and
Fiddle dock. So much enthusiasm is whipped up in this
little book, membership of The Wildlife Trusts and other
conservation groups should flourish.

The armchair adventurer may even be inspired to
discover the real outdoors.

Valerie Elliott, *The Times* Countryside Editor

WHERE HAVE ALL THE SPARROWS GONE?

Once viewed as so common that conservationists didn't have to worry about it, the house sparrow has suffered a mighty decline in recent years. Learned juries are still out on why this may be, but several theories are being explored:

Intensive farming – modern agricultural practices have reduced the amount of food available to birds during the winter.

Mobile phone masts – the rise in popularity of the mobile phone has coincided with the fall of the house sparrow population, leading some to believe that electromagnetic waves might be interfering with the bird's ability to reproduce or navigate.

Unleaded petrol – fumes given off by the substance might be hampering the survival rate of some of the sparrows' favourite insect foods.

Pesticides – by killing off aphids, pesticides not only reduce the number of ladybirds that feed on them, but the foodstuff that young sparrows need in their early years.

New building techniques – better insulation in our eaves may be reducing the birds' nesting opportunities.

Cats – the growing cat population tends to be more successful in killing groundfeeding birds, of which the house sparrow is a species.

CRYPTIC CREATURES, PUZZLING PLANTS

Unravel the following:
GANIGHTLE
Answer on page 145

THE FOOTIE FALCON

Soon after the Second WorldWar, a games enthusiast called Peter Adolph put together a few tabletop figures and invented a game that was to capture the hearts (and fingers) of small boys everywhere. But he had a problem. He wanted to protect the name of the game – Hobby – but found that he was unable to gain copyright for a word in such common usage. It was the bird world that came to his rescue. He discovered that there is a small falcon called a hobby, so named the game after the bird's Latin name.

The hobby's generic name is *Falco*, but its specific name comes from the fact that it was once seen as a subclass of buzzard, the Latin name for which is *Buteo*. Thus it was that the hobby, the Subbuteo, lent its name to the most enduring tabletop football game of all time.

NOSTALGIC NONSENSE

Readers from the black and white TV generation may remember a children's programme called *Tales of the Riverbank*, in which, *Wind in the Willows* style, three rodent friends carried out their adventures alongside an idyllic flowing river. The programme was narrated by Johnny Morris, and children didn't seem to care that Roddy the white rat, Hammy the hamster and Gordon the guinea pig weren't British anyway.

But then neither was the riverbank itself. The series was shot between 1959 and 1961 in Toronto, although a 1970s follow-up, called *Hammy the Hamster*, was filmed in the Isle of Wight. At the end of filming of the latter, some of the animals escaped, and rumours persist that a colony of guinea pigs made part of the island their own for many years afterwards... perhaps still surviving there to this very day?

7 SPECIES THAT AREN'T WHAT THEY SAY THEY ARE

Little mouse-ear is actually a plant
Wood hedgehog is actually a fungus
Garden tiger is actually a moth
Yellow bird's-nest is actually a plant
Brilliant emerald is actually a dragonfly
Fat hen is actually a plant
Ragged robin is actually a plant
*Incidentally, ragged robin is named not after the bird, but
after the folklore elf Robin Goodfellow, who appeared
as Puck in Shakespeare's* A Midsummer Night's Dream

THE WEASEL IS WEASELLY RECOGNISED, BUT THE STOAT IS STOATALLY DIFFERENT

If only that were the case. Stoats and weasels, as they flash by in hot pursuit of a leveret or rodent, are very hard to tell apart in the wild. Often all you're left with is an image of a brown and white, elongated creature with its legs stretched out before and behind like a tiny cheetah.

The stoat, however, is much bigger than the weasel, on average weighing three times more. Should you catch sight of the tail, a long tail with a black-furred tip will give away the stoat's presence. The weasel's tail is shorter without the black. Along the body, there is a clearly defined line between the brown and white on a stoat, whereas the two colours blur more in the middle on a weasel.

If you see the animal in winter, life gets easier. Stoats grow white coats – ermine – during the cold months, whereas weasels maintain their summer garb.

A WHEEL GOOD TIME

Dragonflies have evolved a complex and sometimes time-consuming position for mating, called the wheel. This is a unique approach in animal mating, because it uses the fact that male dragonflies have secondary genital equipment.

The primary genitals in both genders are in the latter segments of their abdomens – in other words, at the far end of the body. Yet prior to copulation, the male is able to transfer his sperm up the length of his abdomen towards his main torso. He then clasps the female's head with the end of his abdomen, using pincers that are shaped to fit grooves along the side of her head, and if his enticement is successful, she bends her abdomen upwards until the tip of it, where her genitals lie, are in contact with the upper part of his own abdomen, where his sperm now lies; the wheel is formed, and the fun begins.

And what fun it is. Although in some species, copulation can last for just a few seconds, in others the process can last hours, sometimes up to six. It's a fascinating event to watch, but beware: after a few minutes you do begin to feel like a bit of a voyeur.

FROGS ARE FUNNY

A lonely frog goes to a fortune-teller to find out his future. The fortune-teller gazes deep into her crystal ball and peers through its mists. Finally, she looks up. 'You are going to meet a beautiful young girl who will want to know everything about you.' The frog is thrilled.

'This is brilliant! Where will I meet her? At work? At a party?' 'No' says the fortune-teller, 'at a biology class.'

HIDE ETIQUETTE FOR THE UNITIATED

Nature hides have a code of their own, which can make them quite intimidating to the newcomer. Here are six tips to help you avoid looking like a wildlife virgin:

1. Don't stick your arm out of the window while pointing at the pretty little duck
The reason that hides exist is to fool the wildlife into thinking that they're alone in their environment. Waving arms and pointing fingers can destroy the illusion, as well as your own credibility. Leaving the door open once you've gone in can do the same.

2. Keep quiet
Sotto voce is a good motto – this isn't a zoo, after all. Not only might your raised voice disturb the wildlife, it can also be an irritating interruption to the gentle contemplation of nature being enjoyed by the other occupants of the hide. Keep your voice down as you approach the hide, too.

3. Don't pretend to be David
While you're sitting there watching the birds and animals, and surrounded by whispering adults, you must resist the temptation to do a David Attenborough. The urge wears off after about your third or fourth visit, so if you do break into a breathless 'And out here, just in front of me, one of nature's most enigmatic creatures is about to perform a dance rarely seen by the human eye', then you've given yourself away.

4. Don't clutter the place up
Leaving your rucksack, thermos flask, ID books and bag of goodies from the gift shop strewn on the seats means that you might be stopping someone else from enjoying the view. In addition, that space between the benches is not a handy storage area for carrier bags, it's a viewing point for wheelchair users.

5. Don't worry about not knowing

Although the camouflaged, equipment-carrying, wisely nodding hordes around you may look as if they'd frown upon the ignorant, if you really have no idea what that little brown job is that's wandering around right in front of you, then don't be afraid to ask. Most nature lovers are delighted to be able to share their knowledge, and you'll probably find out even more about what you're watching than a guidebook could tell you.

6. Stay there

If you've got the time, give it at least 30 minutes. You may feel that you've seen everything from a particular hide within the first five minutes, but part of the great pleasure is the wait for the unexpected appearance, or the sudden change in behaviour. A hobby flashing past as it grabs a dragonfly; a heron quickly stabbing at an eel, the seemingly new view as the light changes across a lake: these and many more delights are seen only by the patient.

SITES FOR SORE EYES

One of the most spectacular geological sites in the country is Earl's Hill in Shropshire. Its main hill, when viewed from one angle, looks like a sleeping dragon, which is particularly appropriate as it was created by fiery layers of lava that burst from the rocks 650 million years ago. In more recent times, an Iron Age hill fort was built on its summit in around 600 BC.

Today, Earl's Hill is a magnificent nature reserve. Its woods of hazel, ash, oak, field maple, holly and yew are awash with bluebells, while dippers and grey wagtails can be spotted flying just along the stream, or bobbing up and down on rocks. The old meadowland contains the hills of yellow meadow ants, while over 30 species of butterfly have been recorded here. In 1964, it became the first reserve to be launched by the Shropshire Wildlife Trust.

DUNROAMIN' NO MORE

If ever proof was wanted that our hearts lie in the countryside, then we can find it in the way we name our homes. Of the 50 leading house names in Britain, according to a recent survey, all bar a handful are based on rural hankerings:

1. The Cottage
2. Rose Cottage
3. The Bungalow
4. The Coach House
5. Orchard House
6. The Lodge
7. Woodlands
8. The Old School House
9. Ivy Cottage
10. The Willows
11. The Barn
12. The Old Rectory
13. Hillside
14. Hillcrest
15. The Croft
16. The Old Vicarage
17. Sunnyside
18. Orchard Cottage
19. Yew Tree Cottage
20. The Laurels
21. The Old Post Office
22. The Gables
23. The Hollies
24. The Beeches
25. The Firs
26. Woodside
27. Meadow View
28. The Stables
29. The White House
30. Holly Cottage
31. Willow Cottage
32. Highfield
33. The Haven
34. Springfield
35. Fairview
36. White Cottage
37. Mill House
38. The Orchard
39. Treetops
40. Primrose Cottage
41. The Granary
42. The Nook
43. Corner Cottage
44. School House
45. Greenacres
46. The Old School
47. Honeysuckle Cottage
48. Lilac Cottage
49. Wayside
50. Oaklands

Not far outside this list come Badgers Cottage, Cuckoo Cottage, Fox Hollow, Magpies, Robin Hill, Squirrels Leap, Swallow Barn and Two Hoots.

ON GOSSAMER WINGS

Gossamer is the name given to the light, filmy money-spider webs that appear in grasses on sunny autumn mornings. The name comes from a contraction of goose summer, ie St Martin's summer, the feast day in November when geese were traditionally eaten. The tiny spiders are able to spin their webs across such great distances by allowing themselves to be wafted along on autumn breezes as they spin.

WILD ABOUT WILDLIFE

When Shakespeare gave Hotspur the line 'Nay, I'll have a starling shall be taught to speak nothing' in *Henry IV Part 1*, he would have had no idea what this allusion was to bring about.

Eugene Scheiffelin was a 19th-century American Shakespeare fanatic with an equally crazy love of wildlife, who found a way to combine his two loves: release each of the 55 species of bird mentioned in Shakespeare into America. He had no real success, except with the starlings. Scheiffelin released 60 of the birds into New York City's Central Park in 1890, and 40 more the following year, and by 1950 the population had risen to many millions, the birds even reaching the Pacific Ocean. By the 1960s, California decided to cull the starlings because they had become such a pest. Over nine million birds were slaughtered, but it was impossible to kill every starling in the state, and numbers soon built back up again.

Today, there are approximately 200 million European starlings in America, a full third of the world's population.

10 SURE SIGNS THAT
YOU'RE A WEREWOLF

1. You wake up naked in a field a couple of times
   a month.
2. You have an unusually passionate hatred of vegetarians
   except with mayonnaise.
3. Your friends call you Hairy McLairy.
4. You have an above-average tendency to bite your
   tongue.
5. You can trace your family tree back to Lon Chaney Jr.
6. Your nose-hair clippers keep breaking.
7. Moonlight becomes you, it goes with your hair.
8. A shop has recently opened down the high street,
   selling silver bullets.
9. Your other friends call you Wolfgang de Wolf,
   or Wolfie for short.
10. You keep finding yourself wondering if Mowgli's
    doing OK.

DON'T BE KOI

Herons are not exactly on the Christmas card list of the
nation's ornamental-fish owners, their predilection for shiny,
easily catchable pond fare driving many a gardener to
distraction. Yet there's one Northampton family whose prize
koi had a lucky and bizarre escape from the hungry bird.

Sitting around their glowing winter fireplace, they
glanced out of the window, and noticed the heron pluck one
of their wriggling koi from their garden pond. In a panic,
they yelled and waved their arms, but too late… the bird
had taken wing and the fish was gone.

But not for long. Perhaps startled by the frantic family,
perhaps unused to the size of the fish, the heron was unable
to hold onto it. As it flew over the house, it dropped it
straight down the chimney and onto the living room carpet.
The heron went hungry, and the fish survived.

THE OWL AND THE NIGHTINGALE

Florence Nightingale, nurse extraordinaire, had a great love of birds. 'There is nothing makes my heart thrill like the voice of birds, much more than the human voice. It is the angels calling us with their songs.' Living in London near the gardens of the Dorchester Hotel, she would happily feed the birds, watching and listening to them: 'There is a thrush here. We fed him during the winter – he is so good as to sing in the trees opposite my bedroom windows, in all the din of Park Lane, the only thrush I ever heard sing in London.' To her childhood home, she wrote asking for the birds to be fed 'as usual, and charge it to me'.

Her writing has even given clues to the fact that the ebb and flow of urban bird populations is not necessarily just a modern phenomenon: 'I don't believe a word of it, that sparrow clubs are at an end and bird slaughter stopped. I saw a sensible diminution of birds in my last few weeks at Claydon over and above the extraordinary disappearance of the last two years. Some species have entirely disappeared. One wretched half-starved starling who came to my window to beg is the sole representative remaining of the splendid crown of starlings which used to sit or parade along the top of your church tower.'

Yet it was for an owl that the Lady of the Lamp devoted perhaps her greatest love. Rescuing it while in Greece from some boys who were tormenting it, she brought the bird back to England in 1850, and kept it with her in her bedroom at night, and carried it around with her in her pocket during the day. She named the owl Athena after the goddess of wisdom whose sacred symbol was the bird (the Latin name of the little owl, incidentally, is *Athene noctua*).

SITES FOR SORE EYES

Cley, on the north Norfolk coast, is a birdwatcher's heaven. Its fresh and saltwater marshes provide feeding, roosting and breeding opportunities for a host of species, while the surrounding area contains habitats as diverse as shingle and dune, mudflats, ancient heathland and deciduous woodland, as well as magnificent vantage points for excellent sea-watching.

The east bank of the reserve is thought by many to be the best birding spot in the country. Not only does it give fine views of wildfowl and wading flocks, but the adjacent pools are frequently host to any number of unusual and passage species. One of the best nature-watchers to recognise its value was the one-time Cley warden and birding legend Richard Richardson, who could frequently be found in the 1940s, 1950s, 1960s and 1970s standing on its muddy path, watching and sketching the birds below and above, and who, as writer Richard Mabey once said, 'had the uncanny knack of being able to see the world from a bird's point of view'.

Cley was The Wildlife Trusts' very first reserve, purchased by the then fledgeling Norfolk Naturalists' Trust in 1926.

CRYPTIC CREATURES, PUZZLING PLANTS

My first is in badger and also in bird
My second's in seen and also in heard
My third is in petal and stamen and leaf
My fourth is in common but never in heath
My fifth is in hornet but never in bee
My whole is a tree that sounds good by the sea
Answer on page 145

BY NAME, BY NATION

There are various practices for naming new dinosaur finds, one of the commonest being the place in which you found it. To date there has been no record of a Grimsbychus or a Sloughraptor, and we can only hope that there might one day be a Llanfairpwllgwyngyllgogerychwyrndrobwyll-llantysiliogogogochosaurus, but in the meantime, the following will have to do:

Albertosaurus...Alberta, Canada
Andesaurus.............The Andes Mountains, South America
Coloradisaurus..............Colorado Formation in Argentina
Denversaurus ....Denver, Colorado, USA
Edmontosaurus ....Edmonton Formation, Alberta, Canada
Indosaurus and Indosuchus ....India
Lesothosaurus ....Lesotho, southern Africa
Utahraptor ....Utah, USA
Szechuanosaurus ....Szechuan, China

MEANWHILE, IN A FOREIGN LAND...

The vast majority of male birds don't have penises, mating by pressing their genitals against the females' in a 'cloacal kiss', but ostriches do have them, measuring up to 20cm in length, as do some ducks. The rather appropriately named stiff-tailed ducks of the Americas were known to have penises that even match those of the ostrich, until...

In September 2001, scientists came across one of nature's truly extraordinary sights: an Argentine lake duck with a 42.5cm penis. This remarkable organ, longer than the bird itself, rests naturally in a corkscrew shape for compactness, and has a brushlike tip at the end, probably to brush away another male's sperm from a female, so great is the sexual competition amongst the species.

Of all the patron saints, perhaps the most famous is the one designated to the animals, St Francis of Assisi.

Francis Bernardone was born at Assisi in Umbria in 1181 or 1182. His father was a successful merchant, and Francis dreamed either of emulating him, or of becoming a noble knight. While following the latter path, he took part in an attack on Perugia at the age of 20, but was captured and imprisoned for a year, during which time he turned to religion.

By his mid-20s, he was devoting himself to the Church, much to his father's shame. Now it was the turn of his father to imprison him, but he did not give up his faith, going on to found a brotherhood on behalf of Pope Innocent III, known as the Friars Minor. They would later become the Franciscans. With his order he travelled Italy, preaching and emphasising the importance of simplicity and poverty. He was joined in 1212 by Clara Sciffi, a rich girl from Assisi who was so taken by his cause that she founded her own sisterhood, the Poor Clares.

Finding the management of men too disruptive, Francis eventually went to the mountains to live among the animals in seclusion and prayer. He died in 1226, and his feast day is October 4.

Not all patron saints had such love of animals, however. St Hubert was a son of the 7th-century Duke of Aquitaine, who loved the chase. One Good Friday, while out hunting a deer, he was amazed to find the stag turning to him, with a cross between its antlers, stating: 'Hubert, unless you turn to the Lord, and lead a holy life, you shall quickly fall into the abyss of Hell!' Hubert did as he was bid, distributed his wealth and turned to the Church. He died some years later while reciting the Lord's Prayer. With a somewhat cruel irony, having renounced his early destructive days, he was given November 3 as a feast day, and the title patron saint of hunters. Incidentally, if your profession is smelter or maker of precision instruments, then he's your patron saint too.

St Patrick, patron saint of Ireland, deserves a mention too, as he was believed to have given a hilltop sermon that rid the country of snakes. There are some who argue that they could have done that, too, seeing as Ireland never had any snakes in the first place, but who's quibbling?

STRANGELY OMITTED FROM THE I-SPY BOOK OF ANIMALS

Catoblepas

(also known as gorgon – not to be confused with its namesake that has a head full of snakes). Admire from distance. If mane rises, flee with reasonable speed, as catoblepas is about to emit noxious fumes that will cause fatal convulsions. Makes poor pet. Score: 40 pts.

FROGS ARE FUNNY

A frog goes into a job centre, hops up to the counter and
asks 'Got a job?'

The man behind the counter looks around for a moment,
then notices the frog down below. 'I beg your pardon,' he
says. 'Did you say something?' 'Sure did,' says the frog.

'Wondered if you've got anything going?' The man is
beside himself. A talking frog!

'Look, why don't you come back tomorrow. I'm sure
I'll have something for you then.'

The frog leaves, and the man is on the phone
immediately, phoning the circus, the TV chat shows, the
newspapers and anyone else he can think of who'll pay
handsomely for this scoop.

The next day the frog comes back. 'So, got a job?' he
asks. 'You bet,' says the man, rubbing his hands. 'I've
lined you up with an exclusive with the *Daily Mail*, your
own TV series, and a long-running job in the circus.
I'll just take the customary 10%. What do you think
about that?'

'Chat shows? The circus?' frowns the frog.

'That's no good. I'm a welder.'

7 GREAT SCRABBLE NAMES

Ouabaio ....an African tree, good for using up vowels
Zyxmyia..a type of fly
Pnyxia..another type of fly
Xyzzors...............................a nematode. Oh, for another 'z'
O-O...a bird
Coccaceae ....bacteria. Clean up on your 'c's
Dixid ....yet another fly

GREAT SCOTT

I had looked forward to helping you to bring him up, but it is a satisfaction to know that he will be safe with you... Make the boy interested in natural history if you can. It is better than games.

These were among Captain Robert Falcon Scott's last written words to his wife Kathleen as he lay dying in a tent in an Antarctic blizzard in 1912. He was referring to his two-year-old son Peter (named after Peter Pan, the creation of his godfather, JM Barrie), who was born on 13 September 1909, the very day that Scott announced his plans to travel south.

Peter did indeed become interested in natural history. Very interested. He became one of the leading conservationists of the 20th century, and the first to be knighted for his work.

Dubbed 'the father of conservation' by David Bellamy, and conservation's 'patron saint' by David Attenborough, Scott founded the Wildfowl & Wetlands Trust, was first chairman of the World Wildlife Fund (now the Worldwide Fund for Nature), originator of the World Conservation Union Red Data Books, and founder of many regional conservation bodies from the Gloucestershire Trust for Nature Conservation to the Falkland Islands Foundation (later Falkland Conservation). He was a prolific wildlife artist, saviour of the Hawaiian goose, and championship-level dinghy racer and skater for good measure. In short, interested in natural history *and* games.

CRYPTIC CREATURES, PUZZLING PLANTS

Unravel the following:
NELT
Answer on page 145

ONCE UPON A TIME

Beasts that walked Britain before cameras were invented

	Last known individual
Spotted hyena	*32,200 BC*
Bison	*25,650 BC*
Woolly rhinoceros	*22,350 BC*
Wolverine	*20,160 BC*
Woolly mammoth	*10,800 BC*
Giant Irish elk	*8960 BC*
Aurochs	*1000 BC*
Brown bear	*Probably 1st century AD*
	although possibly until 8th century AD
Lynx	*180 AD*
Wolf	*1690s AD*

ANIMAL CRACKERS

In 2001, a welder from Huddersfield decided he wanted
to get closer to the birds that lived near his home… so he
turned himself into a walking bird table. Wearing a home-
made construct on his head, he filled it with nuts, and
settled down in some nearby woods. He didn't
have long to wait. Within a few minutes, he heard
a mighty crash, and found himself sprawled on the ground
in agony. The table was shattered in pieces around him,
and a grey squirrel, which had leapt from a nearby tree
onto the makeshift buffet bar, was sprinting off
into the woods. The squirrel ended up with a free meal,
and the welder ended up in a neck brace.

STRANGELY OMITTED FROM THE
I-SPY BOOK OF ANIMALS

Cockatrice

Dragon's body with rooster's head. Prone to killing with noxious breath. Young naturalists might consider carrying a weasel while nature-watching as this is the only animal that can kill the cockatrice, should an individual turn nasty. Score: 20 pts.

A MOLE BY ANY OTHER NAME

Country names for the mole:
Crode
Heunt
Modywart
Mouldiwarp
Oont
Want

HARD TO SWALLOW

Several mysteries of bird migration still surround us, yet at least today, thanks to advanced tracking techniques, we understand the basic principles and routes behind these feats of distance flight. It was not always so. Aristotle believed that redstarts turned into robins during the winter, thus explaining why he saw each species only in different seasons.

More recently, the great 18th-century naturalist Gilbert White also found migration something to ponder. Although aware that many swallows disappeared to warmer climes during the cold months, he also believed that some preferred to hibernate in reedbeds through the winter, or through cold springs, rather than take on the full journey.

'It is worth remarking,' he wrote in 1774, 'that these birds are seen first about lakes and millponds; and it is also very particular, that if these early visitors happen to find frost and snow, as was the case of the two dreadful springs of 1770 and 1771, they immediately withdraw for a time. A circumstance like this is much more in favour of hiding than migration; since it is much more probable that a bird should retire to its hybernaculum just at hand, than return for a week or two only to warmer latitudes.'

POST TRAUMATIC STRESS

It's not just dogs that attack postmen, as this list of
news-making creatures attests:
A goose
A mad cow
A pheasant
A shark (the postie was swimming)
Boo-boo the cat and Yogi the kitten

BACHELOR BOY

The Latin names of British animals and plants are generally descriptive of some aspect of the species, such as location, colour or habit. Yet occasionally a species is given a name based on unusual observations. Such is the case with the common chaffinch, whose Latin name is *Fringilla coelebs* – bachelor finch. Yet when we look out into our gardens or fields and see great flocks of the birds, we tend to see more females than males, particularly in the winter. If these birds are bachelors, it's not for want of choice, so how did the name come about?

The great taxonomist Linnaeus, who worked his way through a system of naming many European species, lived in Sweden, from where many chaffinches migrate south in the winter. They don't go far south, many of them ending up in Britain, but those that do, tend to be female, for this is a species whose genders migrate slightly different distances. Linnaeus noticed that the chaffinches that remained in his home country during the cold season were predominantly male, so bachelor finches they became – much to the head-scratching of those in southern Europe.

8 PLANTS THAT APPEAR TO BELONG TO SOMETHING ELSE

Colt's-foot
Dog's mercury
Dragon's-teeth
Hare's-ear
Leopard's-bane
Sheep's sorrel
Stork's-bill
Viper's-grass
And one that doesn't know WHAT *it belongs to:*
Dove's-foot crane's-bill

ALL GREEK TO ME

In January 2004, a *Guardian* sub-editor accidentally ran
a spellchecker on a series of species' Latin names in
an article on global warming. *Prunella modularis* (the
dunnock) became *Pronely modularise*, the golden toad
became *Buff* instead of *Bufo*, and the Spanish imperial
eagle, once an *Aquila*, turned into an *Alleyway*.
Magnificent.

Why stop there? Here are a few British butterfly species
given a new spellchecked identity:

Ochlodes venata (large skipper) becomes *Occludes vent*
Erynnis tages (dingy skipper) becomes *Reins tags*
Papilio machaon (swallowtail) becomes *Papilla machine*
Colias croceus (clouded yellow) becomes *Coils crocus*
Pieris brassicae (large white) becomes *Piers brassiere*
Pieris napi (green-veined white) becomes *Piers nappy*
Lycaena phlaeas (small copper) becomes *Lycaena phallus*
Cupido minimus (small blue) becomes *Cupid minims*
Polyommatus icarus (common blue) becomes *Polymaths
across*
Limenitis camilla (white admiral) becomes *Laments
Camilla*
Apatura iris (purple emperor) becomes *Aperture iris*
Inachis io (peacock) becomes *Inches ion*
Boloria selene (small pearl-bordered fritillary) becomes
Bolero serene
Melitaea cinxia (Glanville fritillary) becomes *Militia china*
Pararge aegeria (speckled wood) becomes *Prairie auger*
Erebia aethiops (Scotch argus) becomes *Erebus Ethiopia*

CRYPTIC CREATURES, PUZZLING PLANTS

Take the first letter from a British mammal to leave
a beast of burden.
Answer on page 145

THICK THISTLE STICKS

Say the following rapidly and without pause,
and win eternal self-admiration.

A flea and a fly flew in a flue,
Were imprisoned so what could they do?
Said the flea 'Let us fly!'
Said the fly 'Let us flee!'
So they flew through a flaw in the flue!

She sells seashells by the seashore
And the shells she sells are seashells I'm sure
So if she sells seashells by the seashore
Then I'm sure she sells seashore shells

Ann Anteater ate Andy Alligator's apples
So angry Andy Alligator ate Ann Anteater's ants

Thirty-three sly shy thrushes
Said that the sixth sheik's sixth sheep's sick

10 ODDLY NAMED BRITISH MOTHS

The uncertain
The confused
The magpie
The lackey
The iron prominent
The true lover's knot
The Hebrew character
The old lady
The angle shades
The Mother Shipton

27

MEANWHILE, IN A FOREIGN LAND...

Climate change could be the doom of many a creature, as prehistory teaches us, but the threat it poses to the alpine water skink is more unusual than most.

The skink bears its young live, but unlike other live-bearing creatures, the sex of the young is determined by the temperature in which the pregnant female lives. The warmer the environment, the more likely the off-spring are to be male, up to about 32°C (90°F), at which not a single female is born.

Living as it does in alpine areas, the water skink's habitat temperature is therefore at just the right balance to produce the optimum percentage of male and female young. Yet if predictions are correct, and the region warms up in the coming decades, then the female water skink may become a thing of the past... as would the species.

WILL YOU GET THE BILL?

Beak or bill: which is the correct name for each bird? If you want to play it safe, go for beak each time, as this is the actual name given to the skull extension that all birds have. Beaks owned by web-footed birds and pigeons, as well as those that are particularly long, slender or flattened, tend to be known as bills.

Of course, if you should decide to kill the bird, then the confusion ends. The Bill is the one who catches you, while the beak is the one who slaps you in jail.

SIMIAN STARS

Cheetah – The chimpanzee who accompanied Tarzan on his adventures. In 1986, Maureen O'Sullivan, who played Jane, revealed that Cheetah had had the hots for Johnny Weismuller and had to be restrained during her scenes with the actor to prevent sudden bursts of jealousy. She visited him in later life, and he spat in her face.

Marcel – Ross's monkey from the sitcom *Friends*. He was sacked from the series after continual vomiting of live worms on set.

Judy – The chimpanzee from *Daktari*. A close friend of Clarence the cross-eyed lion in the jungle-based animal doctor series, Judy was a trained chimp who responded to up to 75 hand signals. She was potty-trained, although tended to use more toilet paper than necessary.

CJ – The orang-utan who got close to Clint Eastwood in *Every Which Way But Loose*, and *Any Which Way You Can*, and closer still to Bo Derek in *Tarzan, The Ape Man*. Born at Dallas Zoo in 1971, he was put up for adoption at the age of seven when he was purchased by Boone Narr, a head animal trainer and Bill Gage. He liked cookies and milk before going to bed. Reportedly, CJ received a yearly fee of US$500,000.

ANIMAL CRACKERS

Queen Christina of Sweden (1626–1689) had a very strong loathing for fleas. This was particularly unfortunate, as they tended to infest her bedroom. In desperation, she had built a miniature four-inch cannon, with which she would fire tiny cannonballs at them. Records do not tell us whether she ever hit one.

NATURAL MYTHS

Porcupines shoot quills

Not true. Quills are just specially adapted hairs, and porcupines can no more fire them than you could loose off part of your own barnet at will. Porcupines use their quills as weapons by stabbing them into their enemies, but they are able to release them once stuck into a predator's flesh. Each quill is attached to the porcupine's body by tissue, which is sheared upon impact, loosening the quill for detachment. This could make the creature vulnerable to infection from self-impaled tissue damage each time it attacks – or, indeed, lands on the ground because porcupines frequently fall out of trees – except for the fact that the quills come complete with an antibiotic coating.

WHO'D BE A GLANVILLE?

The Glanville fritillary is one of Britain's rarest butterflies, found on the Isle of Wight. A small colony turned up on the Hampshire coast in the 1990s, but attempts to introduce the species elsewhere have not been successful.

Perhaps it inherited its misfortune from Lady Glanville, who gave it its name. She was a fanatical lepidopterist of the 18th century, who collected hundreds of adults and larvae for naturalists to study. She would be seen beating hedges for 'a parcel of wormes', with an enthusiasm shared by few entomologists of the day. Butterflies were not considered as interesting as other creatures: 'None but those deprived of their Senses would go in Pursuit of butterflyes' wrote one contemporary entomologist.

Indeed upon her death, her relatives successfully voided her will on the grounds that anybody who chased butterflies was clearly not of sound mind.

LEARNING FROM NATURE

Don't get too close to the bombardier beetle. It can squirt rapidfire jets of boiling liquid at its enemies at a very high pressure, although those enemies do tend to be ants, frogs and spiders. Its firing action, however, has got aviation specialists interested. The beetle's unique natural combustion technique – known as pulse combustion – could help them solve the problem of re-igniting a gas turbine aircraft engine which has cut out, particularly at great heights where the outside temperature is very low.

Current research is focusing on understanding the beetle's heartshaped miniature combustion chamber, which is less than one millimetre long. Simulations for a larger chamber around a few centimetres long are being prepared, in which gases are ignited by raising the chamber's surface temperature. It is thought that the beetle's unique nozzle shape might also help the scientists develop more accurate squirting power.

MEANWHILE, IN FOREIGN WATERS

We may be used to the discovery of small
and microscopic creatures new to science, but
how about a creature larger in size than man? In the
Pacific Ocean, some 1220m (4000ft) down, a most
unusual new jellyfish has recently been found. Measuring
up to 3m (9ft, 10in) in diameter, 'Big Red' has arms
instead of tentacles, with which it presumably catches its
food. Yet what does it eat, and why has it bucked the
usual jellyfish trend? No-one's sure yet.
Only one specimen has been caught, and its deep
red pigmentation hasn't allowed scientists to get
a good look at the contents of its stomach yet.

Which of the following is not a type of dragonfly:
Hawker
Chaser
Skimmer
Flicker
Darter?
Answer on page 145

WHAT'S UP, DOCK?

Anyone who's spent any time in the countryside will have experienced the wrath of the stinging nettle. But what actually is happening to you when the nettle attacks?

Each sting is a hollow hair stiffened by silica, with a swollen base that contains venom. The tip of this hair is very brittle and when brushed against, no matter how lightly, it breaks off, exposing a sharp point that penetrates the skin. It was once thought that the main constituent of the sting was formic acid, the chemical used by ants, but although this acid is present, the main chemicals are histamine, acetylcholine and 5-hydroxytryptamine (serotonin). There is a fourth ingredient that has not yet been identified.

Yet while nature takes away with one hand, so it gives with another. Dock, which often grows in the neighbourhood of nettles, contains chemicals in its leaves that neutralise the sting and cool the skin.

32

WHAT WAS THAT BIRD?

The feet that make the shapes in the sand or snow
around you.

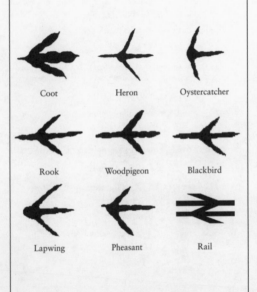

Coot

Heron

Oystercatcher

Rook

Woodpigeon

Blackbird

Lapwing

Pheasant

Rail

11 FILMS THAT EXPLOIT OUR MISCONCEPTIONS OF THE ANIMAL KINGDOM WHILE MAKING A MINT FOR STUDIO EXECS WHO SHOULD REALLY KNOW BETTER

Eight-legged Freaks

Spiders are proven to be man's greatest enemy.

Jaws 3

Having made the point twice before, Hollywood rams home the fact that sharks are man's greatest enemy.

Them

In which man's greatest enemy is revealed to be ants.

The Birds

Man's greatest enemy turns out to be airborne.

Curse of the Wolfman

Man becomes his own greatest enemy with the help of the animal kingdom.

The Swarm

Turns out that man's greatest enemy is an insect after all...

Piranha

...or a fish...

Lake Placid

...or a reptile

Cats and Dogs

Shown to be each other's greatest enemy.

EVER FELT GULLED?

New-year twitches are a staple part of the list-keeping birder's diet. Every year brings the start of a brand-new list, so rarities that have hung around beyond Christmas are worth chasing down as early as possible in January to make sure they appear on that year's list. At Titchwell in North Norfolk, for example, a black-winged stilt, very rare to Britain, has been resident since the early 1990s. Nicknamed Sammy, he has provided birdwatchers of all types with an unusual tick each year – but many like to 'get' him as quickly as possible, just in case poor Sammy pegs it.

Sometimes the new-year twitch doesn't go so well, however. In 2000, many birders decided to see in the new millennium by popping down to Aldeburgh in Suffolk where a graceful ivory gull had been ghosting its way up and down the beach for about three weeks. They'd already ticked him off for 1999, and were now ready to put him on the 2000 list. Sadly, it wasn't to be. The gull wasn't there, frightened off, apparently, by the celebratory fireworks the night before.

THE WILD BUNCH

Original line-up of The Animals in 1963:

Eric Burdon (vocals)
Hilton Valentine (guitar)
Chas Chandler (bass)
Alan Price (keyboards)
John Steel (drums)

NORWEGIAN WOOD...COCK?

In 2003, workers in new, tall glass buildings in the city were noticing an unusual phenomenon. A surprisingly large number of woodcock, a bird of heavily wooded areas, were flying into the windows of their tower blocks. What on earth were they doing there?

Woodcock live in Britain all year round, their superbly camouflaged bodies helping them to blend in with their woodland environment. Usually seen only at dawn or dusk in spring when they make their 'roding' – display – flights, these secretive birds barely make a sound, except the occasional soft grunt. Yet in the autumn, their numbers are augmented by migrational arrivals from the Continent, some from as far away as Scandinavia. Woodcock are rather chunky, so the northern arrivals are probably exhausted by the time they arrive, and fail to notice that new buildings have been erected in their usual flight paths.

This knackered state also makes the usually elusive woodcock easy to approach, an unfortunate state for a gamebird to be in, as Gilbert White, the great 18th-century naturalist, noticed. 'At present I do not know anybody near the seaside that will take the trouble to remark at what time of the moon woodcocks first come,' he wrote. 'If I lived near the sea myself I would soon tell you more of the matter. One thing I used to observe when I was a sportsman was that there were times in which woodcocks were so sluggish and sleepy that they would drop again when flushed just before the spaniels, nay, just at the muzzle of a gun that had been fired at them.'

It seems that woodcocks and buildings are a bad mix in other parts of the world, too. The lakefront at Chicago has had more than 26,000 fatalities from birds flying into buildings over the last 20 years, no fewer than 500 of them being American woodcock. Oddly enough, most of them were female, and studies showed that their ovaries were highly developed, meaning they were just about to lay eggs. It has always been believed that American woodcock mate and lay their eggs in more or less the same place, but the Chicago data suggests that perhaps the females migrate elsewhere for the laying – until the buildings get in the way.

Meanwhile, in Toronto, advice has been put out on how to handle a stunned woodcock should you find it at the foot of a building. Whereas most birds can be put into a bag or box and taken to the vet, the Toronto wildlife centre points out that woodcocks can fly straight upwards, even in a small place, and recommends that a second paper bag be put on top of them to avoid injury to both bird and carrier. And don't forget to put some air holes in.

NATURAL SAYINGS FROM AROUND THE WORLD

The beetle in his hole is a Sultan – Egypt
Before fording the river, do not curse the alligator's
mother – Haiti
He who marries a wolf often looks towards the forest –
Basque
Friends tie their purses with a spider's thread – Italy
The interested friend is a swallow on the roof – France
It is not enough for a man to know how to ride,
he must know how to fall – Mexico
In the ant's house, dew is a deluge – Iran
Only an owl knows the worth of an owl – India
One crow never pecks out another's eyes – Romania
Only the nightingale can understand the rose – Bulgaria

ARTHEI TEKINTHAPIS

Scientists take their jobs very seriously. But sometimes, just sometimes, they let the mask slip. Here is a list of Latin names given to creatures whose discoverers were in a more flippant mood than usual at the time:

Agracadabra..a carabid

Apopyllus now ....a spider

Ba humbugi ....a Fijian snail

Cyclocephala nodanotherwon ....a scarab beetle

Dissup irae................................fossil fly, very hard to see

Eubetia bigaulae ....a moth, yes it is, you betcha by golly

Ittibittium ....a tiny mollusc

Heerz lukenatcha ....a braconid

Kamera lens ....a protist

La cucaracha ....a pyralid

Notnops, Taintnops, Tisentnops .... spiders

They were originally in the genus *Nops*, but were
separated out into these new genera in 1994

Pieza kake ....a fly

Ptomaspis, Dikenaspis, Ariaspis ....types of fish

Remove the '-aspis' to get it

Tabanus rhizonshine..a horse fly

Verae peculya ....a braconid

Vini vidivici ....a parrot

Ytu brutus..a water beetle

SITES FOR SORE EYES

It's summer, the sun is shining, and you want to see a swallowtail butterfly. Understandable. The place to go is Hickling Broad, restored in 2001 by the Norfolk Wildlife Trust, and now one of the finest open water reserves in the country. A short boat ride to the new 18m (60ft) Tree Tower provides excellent opportunities for watching other wildlife, too, including roving marsh harriers, sizeable flocks of wildfowl, and the chance of a glimpse of the secretive bittern.

Look out too, as you take the Water Trail, for the local Norfolk hawker dragonfly, one of the reserve's specialities, as well as rare species of stonewort and marsh orchid. The Broads are the reminder of different times, the water-filled pits the remnants of hand-dug peat excavations, used as fuel in the Middle Ages. But today, the Broads are home to milk-parsley, the foodplant of the rare swallowtail butterfly with its soaring courtship flight and magnificent wingspan.

FROGS ARE FUNNY

A chicken walks into a library, goes up to the counter and clucks 'book, book, book'.
The librarian is bemused, but hands over three books without thinking. The chicken tucks them under its wing, and waddles out. The next day it's back – 'book, book, book' – and the next, and the next, each time going off with three books.
By the fifth day, the librarian is so curious, he decides to follow the chicken. He follows it down the road to the pond on the village green, where he watches the chicken hand the books over to a frog, who leafs through them croaking: 'Reddit, reddit, reddit'.

SAY THAT AGAIN?

Recognising birds by their calls takes experience, but there are a few short cuts. Some species have such distinctive calls that they've been translated, so to speak, into English, such is their familiarity. Here are a few of the best known:

Wet my lips..Quail
A little bit of bread and no cheese ....Yellowhammer
Go back, go back ....Red Grouse
Take two turns, Taffy.......................................Woodpigeon
Tree, tree, tree, once more I come to thee ....Pied Flycatcher
Nevermore ....Raven (according to Edgar Allan Poe)

CRYPTIC CREATURES, PUZZLING PLANTS

My first is in eagle but never in hawk
My second's in speaking but never in talk
My third is in dove but never in pigeon
My fourth is in teal and also in wigeon
My fifth is in throne and also in crown
My whole is a bird that can sure get you down
Answer on page 145

MEANWHILE, IN FOREIGN WATERS...

The sailfish is considered to be the fastest fish in the world over short distances: it has been recorded travelling at 68mph. Growing up to 3m (10ft) in length, it can lay as many as 4.8 million eggs in one breeding season.

WHAT'S SO LADYLIKE ABOUT
THE LADYBIRD?

Of the thousands of species of ladybird found around the world, over 40 can be regularly seen in Britain, of which 26 are recognisable as ladybirds. Often named after the number of spots on their wing-cases (elytra), the vast majority of our species are carnivorous, their food of choice being aphids, which make them gardeners' favourites. The vegetarians feed on mildews.

Many insects are brightly coloured as a means of warning predators that they're not particularly good to eat – a sort of wildlife danger symbol – and ladybirds are no exception. They use a defence mechanism known as reflex bleeding, releasing drops of their pungent blood from their legs onto the tongue or beak of their devourer. This does little good to the individual that gets chomped, but its predator will think twice before feasting on ladybirds again. The average ladybird will consume 5500 aphids in its year-long life.

So what's so lady-like about all this? The insect's red body reminded many of medieval paintings depicting the Virgin Mary wearing a red cloak, while the spots of the common seven-spot ladybird were seen to represent her seven joys and seven sorrows. Add in the fact that the insect can fly, and 'Our Lady's bird' became its early vernacular name.

THE BOTTOMLESS PIT

Ant-lions were first reliably recorded in Britain in 1931, but it is only in more recent years that the creatures have been more regularly sighted, principally on the East Anglian coast.

Ant-lion is the name given to the larvae of the *Myrmeleontidae* family, insects that resemble small damselflies in flight. The larvae corkscrew themselves backwards into sand, leaving a funnel-shaped pit above them. There they lie in wait with just their pincers showing. Passing insects fall into the pit, and struggle to get out due to the loose sand grains that make the pit wall. Sometimes, while on the edge of the pit, they are bombarded by sand flicked at them by the ant-lion's head, until they lose their footing and fall in.

Once its prey is at the bottom of the pit, the ant-lion grabs it with its pincers and proceeds to infuse enzymes into its body. These enzymes kill the insect, and dissolve its soft tissue into liquid, which the ant-lion then sucks.

Because the larva digests its meal so efficiently, it has no need of an anus, bringing up any residual solids as a pellet once it turns into an adult.

CRYPTIC CREATURES, PUZZLING PLANTS

Take the first letter from a dog to leave a bird of prey.
Answer on page 145

MEDIEVAL MAGIC

How to pronounce the first 12 lines of Chaucer's
beautiful introduction to *The Canterbury Tales*:

Whan that Aprille with his
shoores soote/*Wan thot
A'prill with his sure-es
so-tuh*

The tendre croppes and the
yonge sun/*The tawn-dray
crop-pays and the young-
gay soan*

The drought of March hath
perced to the roote/*The
drewgt of March hath pear-
said to the row-tuh*

Hath in the ram his halve
cours yronne/*Hath in the
rahm his hall-vey coors
e-rown*

And bathed every vein in
swich liquor/*And ba-thed
every vane in sweech
lee-coor*

And smale fowles maken
melodye/*And smal-ay
foe-lays mock-en mel-oh-
dee-uh*

Of which vertu engendred
is the flour/*Of wheech ver-
too en-jen-dred is the flu-er*

That slepen all the night
with open eye/*That slep-en
all the neekdt with open
ee-ah*

When Zephyrus eek with
his sweete breeth/*When
Zeph-er-us ache with his
sway-tuh breath*

So priketh hem nature in hir
courages/*So prick-eth him
nahtour in hear core-ahj-ez*

Inspired hath in every holt
and heeth/*In-spear-ed hath
in every holt and heth*

Thanne longen folke to
goon pilgrimages/*Thah-nay
lon-gen folk to goen-on
pilgrim-ahj-ez*

MAYBE ITS MOTHER LOVES IT

Quite possibly the hardest of Britain's creatures to harbour feelings of fondness for is the hagfish. This curious sea creature resembles a pinkish or grey-ish eel, with short tentacles around its mouth, and glands along its side. For a couple of hundred million years, the hagfish has cheerfully lived out an existence chewing its way into the bodies of ill or dead fish or marine worms, and eating its way out again.

The glamour doesn't stop there. Try catching a hagfish, and you'll find out what the glands are for: they secrete copious amounts of mucus-like slime that has most predators gummed up in the mouth, or recoiling in horror. The hagfish is even capable of sneezing out slime from its mouth.

Should you happen to capture one, however, and slip it into a bucket, don't turn your back. The hagfish is capable of tying itself into a knot, which it uses as a balancing base to force itself over the top of the bucket. Thanks to its slippery body, it then simply slides itself out of the knot again, and makes a break for freedom.

Hard to love, impossible not to admire.

FILMS FOR WILDLIFE-WATCHERS

The Mouse that Roared (1959)

Sweet Bird Of Youth (1962)

The Birds (1963)

Cat Ballou (1965)

Paper Lion (1968)

SITES FOR SORE EYES

The Isles of Scilly are like nowhere else in the world: a microcosm of diversity, a unique way of life, and a beautiful, unspoilt natural environment. Auks, petrels, shearwaters and fulmars breed around the archipelago, while bats, which do not hibernate due to the warm climate, can be seen feeding all year round.

The sea life is, of course, impressive. Porpoises, dolphins and the occasional whale are to be looked out for, along with the spectacular sun fish, easily seen as the water is so clear around the islands. Land-based mammals are few and far between, but the eastern isles are very good for seals, and if you're very lucky, you might catch a glimpse of the endemic Scilly shrew. The heady scent of the narcissus crop fills the winter air, while three types of adder's-tongue fern grace St Agnes Island. The four inhabited islands can be explored via a series of permissive paths, and the whole natural spectacle is looked after by The Isles of Scilly Wildlife Trust.

REAL JOBS HELD BY JOHNNY MORRIS

Many young children of the 1960s and 1970s grew up believing that Johnny Morris was a zoo-keeper, rather than a TV presenter. His show, *Animal Magic*, featured a host of creatures that appeared to have conversations with Johnny as he sat with them in their cages. But his Dolittle act came relatively late in life.

Before the days of *Animal Magic*, he had been a:

Solicitor's assistant
Timekeeper on a building site
Salesman
Farm manager in Wiltshire
Hot Chestnut Man – telling yarns on TV in the 1950s

A NEW SPECIES

The rare five-legged elephant that
has scientists baffled.

OUT WITH GOUT

Meadow saffron is one of the oldest medicinal plants still
in pharmaceutical use today. Its ability to help treat joint
pains was recorded as far back as 100 AD, and today its
active alkaloid constituent is recognised as a valuable
drug, colchicine, for the treatment of acute gout.

WHY FUNGI AREN'T PLANTS

- Fungi cell walls are made of chitin, not cellulose as in plants.
- Fungi have no chlorophyll so cannot make their own food.
- Fungi digest food outside their bodies by excreting enzymes that ooze out of the fungus body, and then absorb digested material through the cell walls.
- Fungal cells are simple in structure and function: most are tubular in shape, connected end to end and thereafter deploy as circular growths of hairlike material.
- Fungi reproduce by producing spores which are little more than a fragment of the parent fungus cell.
- Fungi have no roots, stems, leaves or bark.

As a result of these and other differences, biologists created a third kingdom of living organisms – the Fungi *– in 1784. Previously, biologists such as Linnaeus had lumped them together with plants.*

DEFYING GRAVITY

The treecreeper is a mouselike bird that hops its way up the trunks and branches of trees using its long curved bill to pick out insects and larvae from its bark. It's a delightful sight as it hops in a spiral, investigating as it goes, before flying off to try another tree. Then as you're watching it hop along the underside of the branch, you suddenly wonder – why doesn't it fall off? The answer is that as it makes each jump upside-down, it briefly flaps its wings, propelling itself back up to the branch again, although the movement is almost imperceptible to the human eye.

LUCK IN BLACK AND WHITE

One for sorrow
Two for joy
Three for a girl
Four for a boy
Five for silver
Six for gold
Seven for a secret never to be told
Eight for Heaven
Nine for Hell
Ten and you'll meet the Devil himself

This counting rhyme of magpies dates from the belief that members of the crow family brought luck in varying degrees, probably due to their generally black plumage. The disappearance of ravens from the Tower of London, the appearance of a crow on the roof of your house, the sight of crows nesting together, are all apparent signs of impending doom.

The fact that different numbers of magpies can bring alternative results in your life (three means the birth of a girl, four a boy, for example), is likely because of their pied colouring, a roughly even mixture of black and white. Many people today still blink when they see one bird, to turn that single bird into two sightings and bring joy.

Today, magpies have become increasingly common birds in town and countryside. Looks as if we'll all be meeting up with the Devil, then.

YOU'RE SURE OF A BIG SURPRISE

Whereas most British birds somehow vaguely look as if they belong to this country, the golden pheasant is a species that simply oozes international roots. Admitted to the British list in 1971, thanks to its successful colonisation from escaped individuals, it can be found in around half a dozen sites in Britain, chiefly in East Anglia, the South Downs and areas around Poole Harbour.

It's a beautiful bird, found in dense, dark woodland (it roosts in trees at night), the closest it can get to its native Chinese bamboo plantations. The male is unmistakable: very brightly coloured with a yellow crown and lower back, dark wings and upper neck, red underparts and long finely barred tail. Although attempts have been made to introduce it to Europe, only the British population, an accidental introduction, has succeeded. Another species, the Lady Amherst's pheasant, has also taken root, this time in Bedfordshire.

Interestingly, our own pheasant is not an original native of Britain, but was first introduced as a game bird from Asia in around the 12th century.

FROGS ARE FUNNY

A man walks into the doctor's with a frog attached
to his head.
'Good Lord,' says the doctor. 'How on earth did you get
this awful condition?'
'No idea, doc,' says the frog. 'It started as
a wart on my bottom.'

TRUE VISIONARIES

The history of telescopes and binoculars

3500 BC

It was while cooking their local wildlife on sand that Phoenicians first discovered how to make glass. Sadly, no-one was able to use this discovery to help them watch wildlife for another 5000 years, so they just kept on cooking it instead.

1608

The Dutch spectaclemaker Hans Lippershey is generally credited with the invention of the telescope, probably three or four times magnification, but it wasn't until the following year that the Italian scientist Galileo Galilei introduced the concept to astronomy, using his own telescope to see the craters of the moon, and discover sunspots, the rings of Saturn and the moons of Jupiter. His creation gave him a magnification of 30 times.

1825

It may seem strange, but it was over two centuries until someone thought of the idea of combining two telescopes into one optic instrument, thus improving on the limitations of monocular vision. Less strange is the fact that they were called binoculars: it was JP Lemiere who first patented the invention in this year.

1855

AS Herschel is believed to have invented a stereo-telescope in this year, an instrument with two telescopes, each with its objective directed to an eyepiece via mirrors or prisms for a greatly enhanced depth perception.

1894

The German optical industry began to kick off with great success, producing the first high-quality modern binoculars based on the work of optical designer Ernst Abbe, glassmaker Otto Schott and instrument maker Carl Zeiss.

1935
Alexander Smakula helps invent antireflective coatings, increasing binocular light transmission by 50%.

1954
Tele-objective systems (two lens elements separated by air) are introduced, leading to smaller binoculars and improved image quality.

Late 1990s
People began to realise that by combining their digital cameras and their tele-scopes, they could get great photos of wildlife vast distances away, and the digiscoping industry is born. Today, we can watch and take photographs of wildlife without disturbing it, proudly displaying our results without having to shoot, trap, collect and stuff the creatures. But, of course, we're still cooking many of them.

GONE DOWN IN NATURAL HISTORY

Wildlife named after leaders
Caligula – a moth
Jenghizkhan – a dinosaur
Paroxyna cleopatra – a fruit fly
Parides montezuma – a swallowtail
Mammuthus jeffersonii – a mammoth. Named after
US President Thomas Jefferson
Mandelia – a sea slug. Named after Nelson Mandela
Anophthalmus hitleri – a blind cave beetle. It was named
in the 1930s by an admirer of Hitler. Today, it is
very rare because collectors of Nazi memorabilia
seem to think they need one
Sequoia – the redwood. Named after Cherokee
chief Sequoyah
Spartacus – a leaf bug
Washingtonia – a fan palm

THE ROMAN GAMES

Ever wondered why both the animal and plant kingdoms boast families of fritillaries? The word comes from the Latin *Fritillus*, meaning dice box, and the shape of the fritillary flower bears a strong resemblance to the dice boxes used in Roman times. As the flower has a chequered pattern, the butterfly then probably got its name from its similar markings.

There are some, however, who believe that the butterfly, which has a bouncing, fluttery flight, was so named because it flies like the dice as they bounce around in the box. There are others, too, who believe that the flower gained its name not so much from the shape of the dice box, as the spotted nature of its contents. Yet another group prefers to translate *Fritillus* as chequerboard, arguing that both flower and butterfly look like one. What is certain, however, is that each family name has its roots in the games of old Rome.

KNOW YOUR BATS

If you picked a random name from the world list of mammal species, you'd have a 25% chance of coming up with a bat. In Britain, we have 15 species and a couple of occasional visitors, although telling them apart is one of the hardest aspects of nature-watching.

Technology is helping, however. Bat detectors, which measure the frequency of bat calls, are revolutionising bat recording and monitoring. In the early days, they simply converted the high-frequency calls into sound, which still meant you needed to know what you were listening to. Today, you can get detectors that produce visual sonographs of the sound, telling you which species you caught a brief glimpse of as it flicked by. Thanks to this technology, the common pipistrelle was split into two different species in 1995. One emits sounds at 55kHz, the other at 45kHz.

LEARN THE LINGO

Serious birders have found ways of shortening many species' names for easy conversation, and rapid paging and texting of information. Here are some abbreviations:

Barwit Bar-tailed godwit. Black-tailed godwits are known as 'Blackwits'.

Blackback Either of the greater or lesser black-backed gulls.

Capper Capercaillie. The abbreviation shows the correct pronunciation of the first half of the bird's name.

Commic Either common or arctic tern, two species that are notoriously difficult to separate.

Fly Flycatcher. Spotted flycatcher is abbreviated to spot fly.

Greatspot Great spotted woodpecker.

Gropper Grasshopper warbler.

Icky Icterine warbler.

Mickey Ringo Little ringed plover.

Millow Marsh or willow tit. These two birds were recognised as different species only in 1897.

P G Tips Pallas' grasshopper warbler.

Razormot A collection of guillemot and razorbills.

Ringtail A female or immature hen or Montagu's harrier.

Sand Any of the many species of sandpiper.

Sprog House sparrow.

Twitcher Type of birdwatcher who travels great distances to see rare birds at the drop of a hat. Few birders call themselves twitchers, so this term can cause great offence.

SITES FOR SORE EYES

Sometimes an entire island can become a naturalists' paradise, and the Isle of Eigg, of the Inner Hebrides, is no exception. Accessing the island by ferry, visitors have a reasonable chance of watching minke whales as they cross between the months of July and September. On the island itself, wildflower meadows, hazel woods and heather moors open up, while the craggy outline plays host to eagles.

This is one of the great joys of the island: so many habitats within such close walking distance of each other. The bird list is just short of 200 species – impressive for such a small isle – and the plantlife is rich, including 12 species of orchid and 20 nationally rare bryophytes. With otters, 18 species of butterfly, the pygmy shrew and the island wood mouse, brought over by the Norse raiders, Eigg, now co-managed by the Scottish Wildlife Trust, offers a stunning variety of sights and discoveries.

THE VULGAR TONGUE

The word 'vulgar' may have derogatory connotations today, but its root lies in the Latin for 'common', back in the empirical days when to be common was, well, a fairly derogatory thing to be. As a result, many of our most beautiful plants and animals rejoice in scientific vulgarity, even though some are not as 'vulgar' as they used to be:

Polygala vulgaris	Common milkwort
Clinopodium vulgare	Wild basil
Sciurus vulgaris	Red squirrel
Primula vulgaris	Primrose
Sturnus vulgaris	Starling
Echium vulgare	Viper's bugloss

Red deer are among nature's greatest recyclers. There are few waste materials that they do not put to good use.

For a start, there's the velvet. This is a blood-rich skin that encourages summer antler growth. Once the antler has grown, the velvet rubs off, revealing the sturdy antlers within. Rather than litter the countryside, the stag often eats the discarded velvet for nutrients.

The following spring, the dead antler bones drop off, velvet reforms over the stub, and the process begins anew. In the peat-filled Scottish Highlands, stags gain extra nutrients such as calcium and phosphorus from chewing their discarded antlers.

Birthing of young calves begins in late May and continues through to late July, with the majority of calves being born in early to mid-June. After the placenta has been expelled, the hind will eat it and clean any traces of the birth from the area, to minimise the risk of attracting predators.

Still mindful of these predators while suckling her calf, the hind will eat its faeces and urine, to reduce the scent of young deer in the area. This is the most dangerous time: 80% of calf deaths take place in the week after birth.

FILMS FOR WILDLIFE WATCHERS

The Lion in Winter (1968)

The Eagle has Landed (1976)

The Deer Hunter (1978)

Raging Bull (1980)

ANIMAL CRACKERS

In August 2003, Benny Zavala of California was jailed
for 50 days for murdering a government spy. To be more
specific, he thought he was murdering a government spy.
It was actually his daughter's pet guinea pig.

He had thought the pet's teeth were bar-coded
and that there was a camera implanted in its head.
The subsequent trial for cruelty to animals revealed
that Zavala's excessive methamphetamine addiction
may have had something to do with the illusion.
'It's not often you have someone this paranoid from
using drugs that they think a guinea pig is spying on
them for the government,' summed up Deputy District
Attorney Tom Connors. Wise words indeed.

HUNT DOWN YOUR QUARRY

There's an intriguing relationship between conservation
groups, such as The Wildlife Trusts, and quarrying
companies that extract sand and gravel from the land.
The gravel pits that result, as water fills the quarried
areas, can turn into some of the best and richest wildlife
sites in the country.
Sites such as Lackford Lakes in Suffolk and
Attenborough in Nottinghamshire represent how
borrowed land can be returned with interest, as they
now provide a wide range of habitats for birds,
plants, insects and mammals. Summer dragonflies
and winter wildfowl gatherings are often a major feature
of gravel pits, while at Lackford, for example, rarities
such as Caspian tern and spoonbill may well turn up
during the migration seasons.

STRANGELY OMITTED FROM
THE I-SPY BOOK OF ANIMALS

Leucrocuta

Donkey-sized, with one toothbone that extends around its
entire mouth. Best approached from behind, as it cannot
turn its neck. Excellent mimic. Young naturalists are often
lulled into calling out their name, then hearing it called
back in their own voice, before being eaten.

Score: 15 pts.

CRYPTIC CREATURES, PUZZLING PLANTS

Which of the following is not an African antelope:
Suni, Bongo, Nyala, Zorilla, Oribi, Tsessebe?
Answer on page 145

10 SONGS THAT WERE
ORIGINALLY ABOUT FISH

I Have a Bream ....ABBA
Blenny Lane...The Beatles
Super Grouper...................................ABBA again
I'm a Sole Man ....James Brown
Sprat outta Hell..Meatloaf
Herring my car ....Gary Numan
Guppy Love ....Donny Osmond
I Cod You Babe ....Sonny Anchovy
I'll be Dogfish ....Marlin Gaye
We gotta get troutta this plaice ....The Animals

MEANWHILE, IN A FOREIGN LAND...

The honeycreepers of Hawaii are a complex and versatile
group of birds, yet many are severely endangered, the
introduction of rats and cats to the island, along with
deforestation and the rapid spread of disease, bringing
many of the species to extinction. Much work is being
done to save those on the brink, with the hope that some
of the most exotically named creatures may yet struggle
through another century. As well as conservation issues,
there is the matter of some of the most beautiful names in
the bird world. How could we lose the:

Akiapola'au
Akikiki
Maui Alauahio
Anianiou
Oahu Amakihi
Nukupu'u
I'iwi

Very little hope remains for the Po'o-uli, however.
Only two females and one male remain.

LIKING LICHENS

Lichen conservation and monitoring is rarely reported in the press. Yet the importance of studying these composite plant organisms cannot be overestimated. Lichens are not single organisms, but symbiotic associations between plant and fungus that grow very slowly, and are generally dependent upon unpolluted habitat. Extremely sensitive to light conditions, moisture and temperature, they are hard to relocate, but with care and attention, they can be grown in gardens. The British Lichen Society, in fact, recommends that extra inducements to growth can be introduced; in other words, if you're trying to get some lichens growing in your rock garden, try coaxing them in with coatings of beer, yogurt, skimmed milk or even porridge.

Some species have got intriguing names: white script, goblin lights, arctic kidney, alpine sulphur-tresses and river jelly-lichen being among their number. The latter is now virtually extinct in mainland Europe, but still thrives in several of Scotland's finest salmon rivers.

But beware: lichenology can become a fixating subject. The story was told in 1999 of a woman driver who pulled out of a car park, only to notice that she was being followed. After a while she began to get nervous, and tried to lose her pursuer, but with no success. Deciding to confront the situation, she pulled her Lada over, and the car behind pulled up. A man got out and approached her. 'Sorry to disturb you,' he said, peering over her shoulder, 'but I noticed you had a rare species of lichen growing at the base of your car window. Mind if I take a closer look?'

THE SOUND OF SUMMER HOLIDAYS

Cicadas are associated with holidays in warmer climes, calling constantly from some nearby perch as you sip your sundowner and stare out into the dusk from your whitewashed villa.

Yet you don't have to go as far as the Mediterranean to find cicadas – we've got a species of our own in Britain.

The New Forest cicada is found only in the eponymous area, and its high-pitched song is rarely heard, but it's here nonetheless. First recorded in Britain in 1812, it used to have strongholds in Surrey, but has been confined to the New Forest since the early 20th century. Assumed to be extinct in this country for 25 years, it was rediscovered in 1962, where it holds on in about 26 sites in the Forest.

If you want to hear a cicada, this is what you should listen for, according to specialists Bryan Pinchen and Lena Ward: 'The locating song has one or two short warming-up chirrups of two to three seconds and is separated from the courtship song by a variable length of time. Courtship song can last several minutes, and is produced at a low amplitude before rising progressively to a higher volume, from which it sinks a little in the last few seconds before halting. It is best described as a faint, high-pitched ringing buzz, inaudible to most people over the age of 40, but younger people with good hearing can detect it over distances of 60m or more.'

So if you've got good hearing and you're planning a trip to the New Forest... don't forget the sundowner.

WHAT MAKES THE WILDCAT WILD?

The Scottish wildcat is one of Britain's rarest and most elusive mammals. Its future, however, remains uncertain for many reasons. Habitat loss and persecution are among them, but hybridising with feral domestic cats is also slowly diluting the animal's pure stock.

How, then, can you identify a wildcat as being a genuine *Felis silvestris* and not a *Felis catus* hybrid?

Look at the four stripes on the nape.
They should be wavy and broad.

The dorsal stripe should end at the tail root.

The feet have no white patches.

The rump has no spots on it.

The bushy tail is short with a black tip.

LADYBIRD, LADYBIRD...

When an insect closes its wings behind its back, they fold in a particular pattern, rather as when you close an umbrella, and the spokes inside collapse in on themselves (although in the case of insect wings the role of the spokes is played by veins). Yet ladybirds, as do some other insects, have wings that naturally extend beyond their wingcases, or elytra, and need to be drawn in. How do they achieve this, particularly as they have no muscles in the wings themselves?

Next time you see a ladybird land, watch carefully. The wings get pulled underneath the elytra fairly slowly. This is because the ladybird is raising its abdomen so that tiny bristles attach themselves near the base of the wings, then pulling its abdomen forward, dragging the wings with it. It drops the abdomen again, stretches it back, engages with the next section of wing, and drags that in too, until the wings are neatly tucked away.

DOES WHATEVER A SPIDER CAN

Perhaps it's because his powers are based on an animal himself, but Spider-Man has more than his fair share of creature-based foes. Here's a sample of villains who've been put on ice by the friendly neighbourhood Spider-Man over the last 40 years. (He's also gone toe to toe with Kraven the Hunter, although any hunter who goes around with that moniker sounds, frankly, pretty easy to beat.)

Vulture ....Bald and can fly
Rhino ....Huge, with a horn and super-hard skinsuit
Kangaroo ....Leaps about a lot
Gibbon ....Swings about a lot
Scorpion...Watch the sting in the tail
Doctor Octopus ..Cybernetic arms with pincers in the ends
Lizard ....Ferocious and reptilian
Hammerhead...........Mafia boss with a flat, ramming head
Puma ....Careful of those claws
Tarantula...................................Poisoned tips to his shoes
Beetle ....Little more than a flying thief
Chameleon...Master of disguise
Eel ....Slippery customer
Grizzly ....Big, bad and hairy
Human Fly...Climbs walls. Scary

FILMS FOR WILDLIFE WATCHERS

The Fox and the Hound (1981)

Night Hawk (1981)

Never Cry Wolf (1983)

Gorillas in the Mist (1988)

SITES FOR SORE EYES

There's history aplenty at St Catherine's Hill, the nature reserve near Winchester run by the Hampshire and Isle of Wight Wildlife Trust. It starts with Bronze Age pits, continues with Iron Age ramparts, encompasses Saxon boundaries, and is the site of the Norman chapel that gives the hill its name. Moving to medieval times, look out for the dry valleys known as dongas, ancient trackways that were originally worn away by animal-drawn carts. Up to the 17th century, now, and the 'mizmaze' still stands as a fun feature for children to run around. Even the 20th century has its moment: the site was made famous in the 1990s as the setting for the Twyford Down/M3 protests.

But history isn't all the reserve has to offer: natural history is in abundance, too. Over 350 species of flora adorn this hilly stretch of unimproved chalk downland, including several species of orchid. Look out for the well disguised green hairstreak, while the brown argus, chalkhill and small blue are also among the butterfly contingent. The clumps of beech woodland are home to devil's bolete, while winter brings flocks of fieldfare and redwing.

SO GOOD THEY NAMED IT TWICE

Creatures with scientific generic and specific names that match (tautonyms) include:

Grass snake	*Natrix natrix*
Sole	*Solea solea*
Edible dormouse	*Glis glis*
Otter	*Lutra lutra*
Badger	*Meles meles*
Greylag goose	*Anser anser*
Grey Partridge	*Perdix perdix*
Wren	*Troglodytes troglodytes*

NOT JUST FOR BEETLING ABOUT

There's something about owning a car named after an animal that gets drivers all het up and excitable, particularly in America. Or so it would seem from the number of such vehicles that get churned off the production lines. Here's a list of cars that apparently had a certain type of animalistic driver in mind. Although it makes you wonder about the folk that chose the VW Rabbit.

AC Cobra
Buick Wildcat
Chevrolet Corvette Stingray
Chevrolet Impala
Dodge Ram
Dodge Viper
Ford Mustang
Jaguar
Mercury Cougar
Mercury Lynx
Mercury Sable
Triumph Stag
VW Rabbit
...and Panda car

6 ONOMATOPOEIC BRITISH BIRDS

Cuckoo
Chiffchaff
Hoopoe
Pipit
Curlew
Turtle dove

GONE DOWN IN NATURAL HISTORY

Wildlife named after musicians

Mozartella beethoveni – a wasp.

Fernandocrambus chopinellus – a moth.

Funkotriplogynium iagobadius – a mite. Iago Badius is Latin for James Brown. Funko needs no explanation.

Mackenziurus johnnyi, M. joeyi, M. deedeei, M. ceejayi – trilobites. Named after the Ramones.

Greeffiella beatlei – a nematode worm with a shaggy mane.

Masiakasaurus knopfleri – a dinosaur. The fossil-hunters noticed that they tended to have more success when they played Dire Straits. Knopfler said later: 'the fact that it's a dinosaur is certainly apt'.

Aegrotocatellus jaggeri – a trilobite.

Arcticalymene viciousi, A. rotteni, A. jonesi, A. cooki, A. matlocki – trilobites. Named after the Sex Pistols.

Hyla stingi – a Columbian tree frog. Named after the singer for his work in rainforest conservation.

CRYPTIC CREATURES, PUZZLING PLANTS

Unravel the following:
H
FLY
Answer on page 145

Bird ringing for scientific purposes as we know it today began in Denmark in 1899, but there are much earlier examples of methods of marking particular individuals, as these swallow tales show:

During the Punic wars in the 3rd century BC, nesting swallows were smuggled out of one besieged Ligurian garrison and taken to headquarters, behind the lines. They were then marked and set free, carrying messages back to the front.

A few centuries later, swallows were again used, but this time in betting scams. Betting took place in various places around Italy on the chariot races in Rome, and bets were often still taken long after news of the result was announced in the provinces. Swallows would be taken from these outlying towns to Rome, and released with coloured threads indicating the winner tied to their legs.

In 1250, a German monk told of a swallow that had had a piece of parchment attached to its leg with the words 'Oh swallow, where do you live in winter' written upon it. The swallow allegedly returned the following year with a note that replied 'In Asia, in home of Petrus'.

OUR FEATHERED FRIENDS

Ross's gull
Rachel's malimbe
Say's phoebe
Ardea cinerea monicae – the Mauritanian heron
Acanthiza lineata chandleri – a subspecies of the striated thornbill
...and Joey the parrot

With the exception of membership magazines that are put together by wildlife charities, such as The Wildlife Trusts' own *Natural World*, the general public interested in nature is poorly served by Britain's publishing industry. In amongst the copious newsstand publications on cookery, gardening, cars, DVDs and even body-building, barely two or three wildlife magazines can be found.

There is, however, a magazine to which everyone interested in natural history should subscribe. *British Wildlife Magazine*, published by British Wildlife Publishing, has been sent to subscribers six times annually for the last 15 years. It carries excellent information on all aspects of British nature, from conservation news to regional environmental prgrammes, species accounts to historical and social studies. Its columnists include Peter Marren and Robert Burton, and every issue carries a round-up of seasonal wildlife sightings for the previous two months.

FICTIONAL TALES THAT COULD HAVE BEEN A BIT MORE EQUINE

The Mare of Casterbridge

'Tis Pity She's a Horse

The Bridle of Dracula

Ass You Like It

Donkey Ote

The BFGG

And one that couldn't: *Equus*

TO TICK OR NOT TO TICK

Sometimes, twitchers – the Martinis of the birding world ('Anytime, any place, anywhere') – find themselves in something of a dilemma. Part of the point of twitching is to tick off as many rare birds as possible, so a British first is a must-see. When, in October 1998, news came through that a grey catbird had shown up in Southampton, the twitching world was abuzz. Never had this bird been seen in Britain before. The only problem was, it had come across on a cruise liner, and remained on board the whole time the ship was docked at port.

The agony was rife. Would it be possible to see this mega-tick? Could the ship be boarded? And would it count anyway, as the bird had clearly had some assistance in its trip across the Atlantic. Consciences had plenty to wrestle with. Finally, the liner left port for the Mediterranean, and the catbird finally jumped ship at Malta. All's well that ends well. Another catbird turned up at Anglesey in October 2001, and the species finally joined the British list. Relief all round.

TIPS FOR IN-CAR RELAXATION

As recommended by Kwik-fit fitters everywhere

Juniper helps breathing and concentration.
Mint assists breathing and calm.
Seaweed stimulates mental activity and is recommended in moments of confusion and anger.
Chamomile has calming properties for nervousness.
Fern is a plant with a delicate aroma and relaxing qualities.
Freesia is known for its antidepressant and relaxing qualities.
Grapefruit restores health and enthusiasm and is used to combat difficult moments.

SITES FOR SORE EYES

If you're a jaded city-liver who wants to hear birds singing; if you need inspiration to make your garden work for wildlife; if you've never been to Frog Day; if you would like reassurance that wildlife gardening and city nature conservation can be a giggle, then London's Centre for Wildlife Gardening, in East Dulwich, is the place to visit. Run by the London Wildlife Trust, it contains wild ponds, mini-meadows, hedges, and the cutest little birch woodland, all designed to display the urban heritage of back-yard diversity.

Its information centre is insulated with recycled newspaper pulp, and designed to catch the sun, hold the heat and stay cool in summer. Children can discover wildlife crafts, go on minibeast hunts, learn compost-making and pond-dipping skills and join the summer Eco-Club. Adults, meanwhile, can learn more about how best to garden for wildlife at home.

THE LITTLE GENTLEMAN

In 1702, King William III, otherwise known as William of Orange, was riding his horse around Hampton Court. Sorrel – for that was the horse's name – tripped on a mole-hill, throwing the king to the ground. He died 'from the complications of a fractured clavicle; he developed pneumonia, which complicated his pre-existing heart trouble, and probably suffered a terminal pulmonary embolism' (Clifford Brewer, *The Death of Kings*).

The Jacobites, followers of King James II, who had had their power usurped by the Protestant William, were delighted. It is said that they raised a toast to the 'little gentleman in black velvet' who had given hope to their exiled king – although it was Anne who next ascended to the throne.

SPORTING FLIGHTS OF FANCY

Birdie – a cute little flying creature, or one shot under par in golf

Eagle – a rather larger flying creature, or two shots under par in golf

Albatross – an extremely large flying creature, or three shots under par in golf

Feather – an item for aiding flying creatures, or a boxing weight for small people

Bantam – a creature that can barely fly, or a boxing weight for smaller people

Fly – a tiny flying creature, or a boxing weight for very small people

Bat – a nocturnal flying creature, or a hunk of willow for despatching trundlers in cricket

Duck – a flying creature, or a cricketing occasion when the trundler rapidly gets the better of the hunk of willow

MEANWHILE, IN A FOREIGN LAND...

The higher you pee, the greater your power. This seems to be the message put out by the giant pandas of China, who adopt an intriguing range of positions in order to deposit their urinal scent. In addition to the usual squatting approach, they have been seen cocking one leg, backing up against walls or trees, and even doing handstands as they relieve themselves. It's only the adult males who perform the handstand, and sub-adult males, when sniffing other panda urine, tend to back further away from the higher scent deposits.

Presumably, scent height is an indicator of athletic ability rather than size (unless the younger pandas are fooled into thinking that there are some 20ft individuals out there), and thus competitive advantage. A true case of not wanting to be a little squirt.

HOW TO FIND DORMICE

Dormice are nocturnal and keep themselves to themselves, so are very hard to see. Yet if you put in some decent research during the day, you can increase your chances. Your local Wildlife Trust can tell you which sites to find dormice in your area, but to find specific locations can require some detective work.

First of all, look out for evidence of nests (between autumn and spring only, so as not to disturb). Dormice construct them from shredded honeysuckle bark woven into a ball, often surrounded with layers of leaves. The home is a scruffy, loosely woven structure some 10cm (4in) in diameter, generally fairly close to the ground. Low bramble bushes or thick undergrowth beneath trees with fruit, such as hazel and sweet chestnut, are the best habitats.

Evidence of fine dining is your second clue. Nibbled nuts are worth investigating – a dormouse leaves its hazels with a smooth inside surface, and toothmarks on the outside. Once you've established where the dormice are living, it may be time to lend a hand. Contact your local Wildlife Trust to find out how to encourage them further by putting up nestboxes.

Of course, you may be lucky and find one in your teapot.

BYRD SONG

The 11 members of the Byrds to make appearances on official albums:
Skip Battin • Gene Clark • Michael Clarke
David Crosby • Chris Hillman • Kevin Kelley
Roger McGuinn • Gene Parsons
Gram Parsons • Clarence White • John York

PHENOLOGICALLY SPEAKING

The science of phenology is not new, but in recent years it has begun to grow in importance. It's the study of the effect of changing patterns on naturally regular events, and in particular today, the effect of climate change on seasonal breeding and growth. Spring is one of the key times that phenological change is happening: the mean temperature from January to March in the 1960s was 4.2°C, whereas it stood at 5.6°C in the 1990s. This can have a disturbing effect on wildlife.

• Trees are leafing earlier than usual: horse chestnut shows the greatest advance of 12 days, oak 10 days and ash six.
• Butterflies are appearing earlier: the ringlet in particular is emerging one week earlier for every 1°C that average temperatures rise.

• Birds are migrating earlier: swallows are arriving en masse over two weeks earlier than usual.
• More birds are coming here: several northern European species that usually fly to the Mediterranean in winter are now spending the colder months in a warmer Britain.

STARLINGS MAKE A GREAT IMPRESSION

Starlings are one of the bird species that mimic other bird calls to show off their prowess to potential mates.
Yet some birds have broader repertoires than others, mimicking:
Greenfinches
Magpies
Swallows
Cats
People's whistles
Mobile phones – Nokia is a particular favourite
Ice cream vans

MEANWHILE IN A FOREIGN LAND

The island of New Guinea, second largest in the world, is home to many unusual creatures, but few can match the singing dog. Similar to the dingo, the New Guinea singing dog has a synchronised howl, in which different tones blend with each other. To hear it is an eerie experience. Their bodies are just as flexible as their voices: they can squeeze through any opening large enough to admit their head.

Singing dogs are feral, descended from dogs brought to the island along with human migrations many thousands of years ago. They moved to the mountains, where they developed thicker, slightly longer coats than other wild dogs. In 1948, a pair were captured and brought to Sydney Zoo in Australia, where the breed became internationally famous, and by the 1960s, singing dogs, despite their feral nature, were in high demand across Europe. Today, the breed is endangered in New Guinea, and possibly even extinct, yet in captivity it is still made to sing for its supper. Two individuals even once accompanied opera star Benita Valente on television.

HALF-TIME

The detail that goes into butterfly and moth illustration is extraordinary, and illustrators spend much of their lives peering into microscopes to study colour differentiations, scales and body structure. Yet since the advent of the printing process, help is at hand. Undamaged butterflies and moths are symmetrical, so illustrators only have to complete one side, and let the publishers do the rest. A very handy short cut with over 2500 species in Britain alone to paint.

ANIMAL CRACKERS

Eystein, an 11th-century north Norwegian king, was not a popular ruler. He made it his business to go around the neighbouring regions conquering the people and claiming their land as his own. The people of Throndhjem, however, were sturdier than most, and when Eystein installed his own son as king of their district, they killed him. Furious, Eystein returned to Throndhjem and offered the people a choice: their new king would either be Eystein's own slave Thorer Faxe, or his dog.

The people chose the dog.

Saur, for that was the dog's name, ruled for three years. He lived in a mansion, wore a chain of gold, and was carried around by courtiers, who probably figured they were better off under him than under Eystein. His life ended when he heroically tried to save a herd of cattle from a pack of wolves, and was torn to bits.

SHOPPING THESE DAYS, IT'S A ZOO

Just click on the following to add to your trolley:
Famous Grouse whisky
Woodpecker cider
Penguin biscuits
Bird's Eye fish fingers
Animal biscuits
Doves Farm cereal bars
Fox's glacier mints
Dragonfly tea sachets
Tiger beer
Lyon's tea

NATURE TREK

A useful glossary for when you're discussing wildlife with a Klingon:

bo'Degh – bird, the most general word for a bird-like creature

cha'bIp – a bird noted for its speed

cha'qu' – a bird with a noisy, repetitive cry

ghotI' – fish, most general word for a fishlike creature

jajlo' Qa' – a noisy animal (not a bird) known for making a ruckus at dawn, like a rooster

lIr – a nocturnal bird

lotlhmoq – a bird that swoops into the water in order to catch food, but cannot swim

naHjej – thistle

neb – beak, bill

notqa' – a large, black bird (although nowhere near as large as a *qa'rol*, which is really big)

qanraD – a bird known for its song

qaryoq – bird capable of mimicking speech

Qaj – type of animal with brown lips

Qa'Hom – an animal (not a bird) like a *Qa'* but smaller

raw' – an aquatic bird with colourful plumage

tangqa' – animal species with both genders resembling a bull

toQ – a bird of prey

vem'eq – a bird that feeds almost exclusively on the serpent worm from which *qagh* is made. (Please note that Klingons are not particularly fond of this bird.)

waqboch – a bird with a very long beak

And for the real experts among you:

cha'Do – a species of Klingon bird about which little is known

GONE DOWN IN NATURAL HISTORY

Wildlife named after actors and film-makers

Attenborosaurus – a plesiosaur. Named after David,
the naturalist, not Richard, the *Jurassic Park* actor.

Calponia harrisonfordi – a spider. For his work in
documentary narration. At least it wasn't a snake.

Norasaphus monroeae – a trilobite. The fossil has
a curvy hourglass shape.

*Orsonwelles othello, O. macbeth, O. falstaffius,
O. ambersonorum* – giant Hawaiian spiders.

Rostropria garbo – a wasp. The female of the species
is solitary.

Utahraptor spielbergi – a dinosaur. Discovered mere days
before the premiere of Jurassic Park, this raptor, larger
than any found before, showed that Spielberg's filmic
beasts, derided for their large size, were possible after all.
An extraordinary case of nature coming to
the PR rescue of a film-maker. The dinosaur's name,
incidentally, was not registered properly, and is now
U. ostrommaysorum.

A WILDLIFE RAINBOW

Red fox
Orange footman
Yellow wagtail
Green tiger beetle
Bluebottle
Indigo bush
Violet

YOU'RE SURE OF A BIG SURPRISE

There's something of the Merrie Olde England about the wild boar... but increasingly there may be something of the Merrie New England, too. Reports suggest that there could be as many as 1000 of them wandering and snuffling around the woodlands of south-east England, the offspring of escapees from boar farms that have been husbanding the animal for meat since the early 1980s.

Boar are controversial animals. Weighing up to 400lb, tusked, and faster than the fastest man, they are seen by many to be dangerous creatures if disturbed. Farmers, too, worry that the animals may be powerful enough to break into their fields. Yet wild boars are also wonders for the habitat: their rooting creating shallows, rough areas and extra soil fertility that are ideal for plant growth, while invasive rhododendron populations fall before their snouts.

Should the wild boar be allowed to live in Britain outside of captivity? The jury is still out.

A STOAT BY ANY OTHER NAME

Country names for the stoat

Carre
Clubster
Clubtail
Futteret
Lobster
Puttice
Whitterick
Whutherit

FROGS ARE FUNNY

Two frogs are sitting on a lilypad having a chat. 'You
know what happened to me today?' says one. 'I was
sitting on the bank, just minding my own business,
when I yawned, and a tasty bluebottle flew right
into my mouth.'
'That's great,' says the other. 'But I was even luckier.
I was sitting on the other bank, watching a couple of flies
way above my head, when they bumped into each other
and landed right at my feet.'
An otter swims past. 'Couldn't help overhearing you
guys,' it says. 'But I can top that. I was just lounging
around on the far bank this morning, when a fish leapt
out of the water, cannoned off a passing blackbird,
bounced off a duck's back, and landed
right in front of me.'
'That's extraordinary', says the first frog to the second.
'I didn't know otters could talk.'

SITES FOR SORE EYES

Wordsworth and Coleridge were inspired by the Falls of
Clyde in Lanarkshire, as have been dozens of artists
through the years. Now that the site is run by the Scottish
Wildlife Trust, this dramatic tumble of water with its
surrounding riverside habitat can continue to inspire in the
decades ahead. Peregrine, otter, dipper and badger all make
their home near the river.

Scotland's first public hydro-electric scheme was opened
here in 1927, joined in more recent years by a wildlife
centre. Yet the wildlife itself is what makes the reserve truly
breath-taking: five species of bat fly overhead on summer
evenings; campion, water avens and marsh marigolds adorn
the riverside trail and secretive roe deer are never far away.
Visit in the evenings for accompanied badger-watching.

When Madagascar split away from Africa 165 million years ago, its flora and fauna evolved quite independently from that of the mainland. Lemurs are the best known example of creatures that are endemic to the island, but the largest lemur of all is the most extraordinary. The indri, reasonably common until a century ago, but now numbering only a few thousand individuals, weighs up to 10kg (22lb) and comes down to the ground only to cross treeless areas, or sometimes to eat dirt. Giving birth only once every two or three years, the indri emits an eerie call that sounds human in tone, and is picked up by other indri through the rainforest, surrounding the listener with wailing, childlike howls. Unsurprisingly, many legends exist in Madagascar relating to indris giving birth to human children.

Incidentally, the animal gets its name from the Malagasy for 'Look at that', which is what the first arriving Europeans were told when the lemur was pointed out to them.

10 COLEOPTERISTS (BEETLE-SPECIALISTS) WHO REALLY SHOULD HAVE STUDIED SOMETHING ELSE

Sir TH Beare • WA Beevor • TDA Cockerell
G Crabbe • PC Drake • Sir W Flower
KJ Fox • EA Heath • CG Lamb • JH Leech

And two who were born to the job:
W Lennon and JWH Harrison

STRANGELY OMITTED FROM
THE I-SPY BOOK OF ANIMALS

Manticore
Head of man, body of lion. Observe from side-on – if you stand in front, it will eat you; if you stand behind, it will shoot spikes from its tail at you. Otherwise harmless.
Score: 30 pts.

USEFUL WORDS TO KNOW WHEN
MAMMAL-WATCHING

Den ....stoat home
Form ....hare home
Fortress...complex mole mound
Hoglet ....young hedgehog
Holt..otter home
Jill ....female polecat
Kit..young stoat
Kitten ....young rabbit

HOPPING MAD

When it comes to jumping, the common froghopper – a frequent garden resident that hides its young in a froth called 'cuckoo-spit' – has the others beaten hands down. Only 6mm long, the little insect is capable of propelling its 12mg body 70cm into the air, exerting a force 400 times greater than its own body weight. This compares well with the exploits of a flea, whose force is around 135 times its body weight; a grasshopper, which can manage eight times, and a human, who can get up to about three times.

In addition:
- the froghopper accelerates in a millisecond up to a take-off velocity of 4m/second
- its initial acceleration is 4,000m/second
- the G-force it generates is more than 400 gravities, 80 times greater than that experienced by astronauts
- you need a 2000 frame-per-second camera to record the jump
- the hind legs are so specialised for jumping that they are of no use for walking: the insect simply drags them behind itself.

FILMS FOR WILDLIFE WATCHERS

Dances with Wolves (1990)

The Silence of the Lambs (1991)

The Lion King (1994)

Wag the Dog (1997)

ZOO QUESTION

When David Attenborough started planning *Zoo Quest* in 1954, he was looking for a peg to hang the programme on. Deciding that a search for rare animals around the world would be of interest to viewers, he set off to Sierra Leone in a hunt for the rare bald-headed rock crow, or *Picathartes gymnocephalus*. By the time the first episode aired, the *Zoo Quest* team was able to show film of an array of creatures, from chameleons to starlings, weaver birds to pythons, but no *Picathartes*. At the end of each episode, Attenborough would advise viewers to tune in next week to find out if the bird might appear.

After about four or five episodes, Attenborough was wondering whether the show was successful. Were people interested? One day, he was making his way down Regent Street in London, when a bus pulled up alongside him. The driver rolled down his window. 'Oy, Dave', he shouted, 'are you going to catch that *Picafartees gymno*-bloody-*cephalus* or aren't you?'

Soon afterwards, Attenborough confidently put in a successful bid for a second series.

And yes, they did catch one.

GONE DOWN IN NATURAL HISTORY

Wildlife named after great thinkers

Buddhaites – a mollusc
Confuciusornis sanctus – a dinosaur
Dalailama – a moth. It comes from Tibet
Lutheria and *Marxella* – wasps
Plato – a spider

WHICH MOUSE IN YOUR HOUSE?

House mice are probably the best-known rodent co-inhabitants of our homes, yet the hibernating wood mice and yellow-necked mice are also reasonably common visitors, particularly in the southern counties. House mice are easy to identify – grey all over – but the two woodland species, which are darkish brown with white bellies, need a bit more work.

• The yellow-necked has a collar of yellow fur right across its neck, while the wood often has a yellow chest patch that doesn't join up with the brown fur on its back.
• The yellow-necked is a little larger and noisier than the wood, particularly when caught.
• Out of doors, the yellow-necked prefers mature deciduous woodland, while the wood is more flexible, found in hedgerows, arable fields and, of course, woodland.

SINGING FOR THEIR LIVES

Canaries were once commonly used as guinea-pigs to test whether subterranean mineshafts had breathable air. Today, more technological means are used – where the mines are still in use – but occasionally the canaries still come into their own as saviours of mankind.

The December 2003 earthquake in Bam, Iran, cost the town at least 20,000 lives. The tally was two shorter than it might have been had not rescue workers been drawn to the chirping of two canaries trapped in the rubble. Moving the debris aside, they found two young children alongside the broken birdcage with the still singing canaries. Badly injured, the children were taken to hospital. The canaries were set free.

A MILLENIUM OF INTRODUCTIONS

As Britons colonised the world, so they brought back from their travels plants that have in turn colonised this country. Some botanists, such as Maggie Campbell-Culver, categorise the introduction of plants in 10 phases, some of which overlap:

1000–1560 – plants arrive from continental Europe, due in part to the Norman invasion and the Crusades.

1560–1620 – plants from the Near East, West Asia and the Balkans began arriving.

1620–1662 – botanist John Tradescant brings plants from Russia and the North African coast, and his son does the same from North America.

1660–1720 – the introduction of shrubs and trees from the eastern seaboard of North America.

1680–1774 – plant introductions from southern Africa, especially the Cape of Good Hope.

1772–1820 – the Antipodean period, beginning with the return of Joseph Banks and Captain Cook from the southern hemisphere.

1820–1860 – plants introduced from the west coast of North America.

1840–1870 – plants come from South America.

1840–1890 – arrivals from expeditions to India and the Himalayas.

1890–1930 – plants arrive from China and Japan.

BIG FLEAS HAVE LITTLE FLEAS...

... Upon their backs to bite 'em
And little fleas have littler fleas
And so ad infinitum

Conopid flies have a Ridley Scottesque beginning: their pupae grow, *Alien*-style, inside bees and wasps. The adults lay their eggs inside the insects by grappling with them in mid-air, and injecting the egg into the bee's abdominal cavity between its armoured body segments. Once the egg hatches, the maggot eats its way out.

But even these mini-beasts can be infested. A conopid maggot, already inside a bee, is sometimes got at by pteromalid wasps, which lay a tiny egg inside it (it's hard not to feel sorry for the poor bee at this stage). As the maggot feeds on the bee, so the wasp egg, which hosts up to 40 wasps itself, develops. In spring, out comes the maggot, dying, from which out comes a host of wasps.

MEANWHILE, IN A FOREIGN LAND...

In the early years of 20th-century Argentina, the belief that a family's seventh consecutive son could transform himself into a werewolf was so widely held that such offspring were being abandoned and even killed. To slow down the death rate, a law was passed in the 1920s stating that the president became automatic godfather of seventh sons, thus giving them his protection. The child received a gold medal on his day of baptism, and his schooling was paid for until the age of 21.

The law is still in existence today, and presidents still occasionally attend the baptisms of seventh sons. Particularly in election year.

Next time you're wandering around Middle Earth, see which of the following you can identify. Keep your distance.

Balrogs are evil spirits of fire and were among the first allies of Morgoth in the early days of Arda. Most were destroyed in the wars with elves and men, but a few remain, hidden away in the dark holes of the earth.

Crebain are large black crows that have been corrupted by evil.

Dumbledors are a species of giant wasp with bright black and yellow markings. Easily irritated, these insects have been known to swarm without provocation.

The giant eagles of Middle Earth are the greatest of all birds, nearly 12ft tall with a 35ft wingspan.

Ents (or the Onodrim) are huge plantlike humanoids who appear to be trees at a cursory glance. Although the oldest of the speaking races, the ents were taught by the elves how to become mobile. They now act as caretakers of the forests and wild places.

Fell beasts resemble two-legged dragons with heads much like a vulture and two huge batlike wings. The average specimen reaches about 30ft in length, with often a 40-50ft wingspan.

The Flies of Mordor are one of the few forms of life that actually thrive in Mordor. They are hideous creatures, almost an inch long, with the red mark of the Eye of Sauron on their backs.

Hummerhorns are huge mosquitoes, with a wingspan of nearly 4ft, and weighing almost 10lb. Usually found in swamps and boggy areas, hummerhorns are fearless, and have been known to attack armoured knights.

Huorns are treelike beings who live in forests tended by ents. They may look exactly like trees native to their particular forest, but are in fact either trees awakened from their sleep by ents, or ents who have slipped into dormancy.

Mearas are noble horses that live in the wilds of Middle Earth, occasionally serving as steeds for great lords. When urged to ride hard, they can cover nearly 25 mph for up to 12 hours.

Mewlips are cannibalistic spirits that haunt mortals, feeding on their flesh and blood. They have horribly hunched backs, slanted eyes, sharp claws and teeth, and glistening brownish-grey skin.

Mumakil (sometimes called Oliphaunts) are huge, elephantlike beasts trained by the Haradrim as war beasts.

The great spiders of Middle Earth are truly monstrous creatures, possessing a high degree of sentience, and skilled in deception, stealth, and magic.

Trolls were bred by Morgoth in mockery of the ents. Huge, fearsomely strong, and belligerently stupid, trolls are a curse upon any that come across them.

Wargs are huge wolves infused with the power of first Morgoth, and later the Dark Lord. They have black fur, are much more intelligent than normal wolves, and some are even capable of speech.

ALBADROSS

Marine debris can be lethal to seabirds. Contents found in albatross stomachs include:

Fishing net floats
A nine-inch piece of black plastic tubing
Fishing lures
Cigarette lighters
Toothbrushes
Sun lotion bottles
Inhalers
Soy sauce bottles
Toy planes and cars
A plastic dinosaur

THE MARGARET THATCHER
OF THE BIRD WORLD

The nightjar is one of Britain's more enigmatic birds.
Arriving from Africa in mid-May and returning in
August, it emerges at dusk, flitting through the night to
hunt moths and other insects with its wide-open gape,
then disappearing at dawn again as its mottled plumage
blends perfectly with the lichen-covered logs
and branches on which it roosts. Its nighttime call
is an eerie, vibrant churring song.
Unsurprisingly, then, the nightjar was a mysterious
creature to earlier generations. Until the 17th century,
it was still given the name goatsucker, as it was believed
to feed on the milk of livestock.
Indeed, even its scientific name – *Caprimulgus europaeus*
– means 'European goat-milker'. For this reason, the
bird was also called the Puck bird, or Puckeridge, after
the impish spirit of the night Puck, who also was alleged
to be a milk-snatcher.

GONE DOWN IN NATURAL HISTORY

Wildlife named after artists and writers

Microchilo elgrecoi – a moth.
Pseudoparamys cezannei – an extinct rodent.
Arthurdactylus conandoylensis – a pterosaur. So named
because his story *The Lost World* is set in jungle similar to
where the fossil was found.
Draculoides bramstokeri – a spider.
Legionella shakespearei – a bacterium.
Psephophorus terrypratchetti – a fossil turtle. Pratchett's
fantasy world is carried on the back of such a beast.

ANIMAL CRACKERS

According to Sheila Ryan of Ohio, she has a gift: she can talk with animals, and horses in particular. Using a combination of metal dowsing rods and an understanding of spiritual points on the animal's body, she claims to be able to communicate in quite some detail. For example, Ryan was called in to help one rider find out why her horse was misbehaving at a show. After a little chat, she was able to report back that the horse was offended because its owner had been criticising it. The horse clearly felt that it shouldn't be jumping any more, too, because it apparently added: 'I'm older than you think I am'.

The psychologist (that's Ryan, not the horse)makes a pretty good living out of her holistic horse-healing business, but she's quite the all-round linguist. In addition to English and Horse, she's fluent in Dog and Cat, too. She even once had a cosy little chat with a mountain lion.

YOU'VE GOT SOME NECK!

It was once believed that if you walked slowly round and round a tree with an owl in it, the bird would watch you until it had wrung its own neck. Although owl necks can't turn quite that far, they do have the ability in some species to turn virtually 270° in either direction, thus being able to follow you three-quarters of the way round the tree. They can do this because they've got 14 neck vertebrae, twice as many as most mammals (including humans, giraffes, whales and mice).

Owl necks pale into insignificance alongside those of swans, however, which have up to 25 vertebrae. Even the mighty longnecked sauropods of millions of years ago, such as the 22m Mamenchisaurus, had a maximum of 19.

One of the earliest scientific natural history writers of the Arab world was Abu Uthman Amr ibn Bahr al-Kinani al- Fuqaimi al-Basri al-Jahiz – known simply as al-Jahiz – who was born in Basra in 776. As a youth, he worked with his father in the fish market, but his mother felt there was more to him. She gave him a collection of notebooks and suggested he try a career in writing.

He did. Launching with a study on the 'Institution of the Caliphate', he was taken in by the court of Baghdad, where he later moved. He wrote more than 200 works, including *The Art of Keeping One's Mouth Shut*, *Against Civil Servants*, *Arab Food*, and *In Praise of Merchants*, but it is for his *Book of Animals (Kitab al-Hayawan)* that he is best known today, an encyclopedia of seven large volumes.

The book contains an amazing array of scientific information. Al-Jahiz discusses his observation in detail on the social organisation of ants, and animal communication and psychology. He suggested an ingenious way of expelling mosquitoes and flies from a room-based on his observation that some insects are responsive to light. He also observed that certain parasites adapt to the colour of their host, and expounded on the effects of diet and climate not only on men but also on animals and plants.

Al-Jahiz returned to Basra after spending more than 50 years in Baghdad. He died in Basra in 868, when a pile of books collapsed on him in his private library.

NATURAL MYTHS

Lemmings control their population by jumping off cliffs
Not true. Lemming population is, indeed, a very up-and-down affair, following a four-year cycle in which numbers increase by hundreds of percent, encouraging predators, then crash as the predators become too successful. The cliff myth is based originally on the fact that Norwegian lemmings undertake great migrations about once every 30 years, in which they surge across the landscape in their thousands, jumping into rivers and sometimes falling off rocks to their doom through overcrowding, just as wildebeest do in their own annual migration. The myth was given apparent substance by Walt Disney in a 'factual' nature film called *White Wilderness* which showed lemmings leaping off apparent cliff edges. They were, in fact, being herded into a river from a man-made surface.

EIGHT-LEGGED CHAMELEONS

Britain has two species of octopus: the common, which can grow up to a metre in length, and the curled, which can manage about half that size. The common octopus is actually the least common of the two, but can be found in rocky coasts and lower shores in south-west Britain and the western region of the English Channel. A chameleon of the sea, it can change its colour from grey to brown to yellow to green, depending upon its situation. The curled, or lesser octopus can be found in similar habitats, but along the entire British coastline. Its standard colour is a rusty brown, but it can also change rapidly depending upon its background.

Lamb tree

A plant that grows a lamb, attached by the
navel. The lamb lives its short life by eating the
plant that supports it. The lamb itself is mighty
fine eating. While watching other animals,
the young naturalist may wish to chew on its
fishlike meat, and drink its honeyed blood.
Score: 10 pts.

GONE DOWN IN NATURAL HISTORY

Wildlife named after famous people

Mastagophora dizzydeani – a spider.
Named after a baseball player. The spider uses a sticky
ball to catch its prey.

Campsicnemius charliechaplini – a fly. Named for the
tendency of the fly to die in a bandy-legged position.

Baeturia laureli and *B. hardyi* – cicadas.

Bufonaria borisbeckeri – a sea snail.

Strigiphilus garylarsoni – a louse. The cartoonist wrote
later: 'You have to grab these opportunities when they
come along. I knew no-one was going to name a new
species of swan after me.'

Sula abbotti costelloi – a subspecies of Abbot's booby,
(similar to a gannet), although now extinct.

Sylvilagus palustris hefneri – a marsh rabbit. Only Hugh
Hefner could have a bunny named after him.

Godiva – a nudibranch. Nudibranches are marine
molluscs with exposed, or naked, gills.

CRYPTIC CREATURES, PUZZLING PLANTS

Which of the following is not a coastal fish:
Piddock, Pollack,
Lumpsucker, Father Lasher,
Gurnard?
Answer on page 145

Chaos theory has it that if a butterfly flaps its wings in Tokyo there could be an earthquake in California. But how about if it flaps its wings in America, then magically appears four days later in Cornwall – what does chaos theory have to say about that?

The monarch butterfly, one of nature's most astonishing migrants, spends much of its life pootling up or down the continent of America, yet occasionally the odd one or two turn up in Britain, the first sighting being in 1876. For years, it was assumed they had stowed away on board ships – after all, the monarch may be a mighty flyer, but the Atlantic is a far mightier ocean.

Yet in 1968 and 1981, the south-west coast of Britain was visited by monarchs in their dozens, at exactly the same time that several species of American birds, true rarities in this country, also turned up. Could the weather be playing a part? Then in 1995, on one day alone in October, at least 45 individual monarchs were spotted. Unusually, at the end of September that year, three hurricanes had hit the eastern seaboard of the US, resulting in a strong westerly airflow that culminated in a gale in southwestern Britain on 30 September. The air flow was reasonably warm, and travelled at around 30-35 knots, taking four days to cross the Atlantic, a short enough time for the butterflies to survive on their fat reserves. It was shown, conclusively, that it was possible for a butterfly to cross the Atlantic aided by nothing but the weather.

FROGS ARE FUNNY

A man walks into a bar, buys a pint, then says to
the barman: 'Look at this'. He pulls a frog out of his
pocket, and a tiny piano. The frog settles down at the
piano, and bangs out a perfect performance of
Rachmaninov's 3rd. The barman is amazed, but the man
reaches into his other pocket.
'That's nothing,' he says, pulling out another frog, which
he puts next to the first. This new frog breaks into
a gorgeous rendition of *O Sole Mio*, accompanied
immaculately by the pianist frog. Another man comes up.
'Tell you what,' he says, 'I'll put money behind this bar
to keep you in drink for the rest of the night, if you'll give
me that singing frog.' The first man shrugs and agrees,
and hands it over. As the new owner leaves, the barman
says: 'Are you mad, you could have made a fortune with
that singing frog.' 'Not really,' says the man. 'The pianist
is a ventriloquist.'

BEAUTY IS TRUTH

A Bambara poem in praise of the crowned crane, to some
the most beautiful of birds. The crowned crane is the
national symbol of Uganda.
The beginning of beginning rhythm
Is speech of the crowned crane.
The crowned crane says 'I speak'.
The word is beauty.

HOW ANCIENT IS ANCIENT?

We often talk about ancient woodland, but how old does an area have to be to qualify for such a title? The Woodland Trust provides the definition:

'Ancient woods are those where there is believed to have been continuous woodland cover since at least 1600 AD. Before this, planting was uncommon, so a wood present in 1600 AD was likely to have developed naturally. In Scotland, ancient woodland sites are strictly those shown as semi-natural woodland on the 'Roy' maps (a 1750 military survey and the best source of historical map evidence), and as woodland on all subsequent maps, however they have been combined with long-established woods of semi-natural origin (originating from between 1750 and 1860) into a single category of ancient woodland to take account of uncertainties in compilation of the ancient woodland inventory.

'Ancient semi-natural woodland (ASNW) is composed of native tree species that have not obviously been planted. Planted ancient woodland sites (PAWS) are ancient woods in which the former tree cover has been replaced, often with non-native trees. Important features of ancient woodland often survive in many of these woods, including characteristic flora and fauna, and archaeology.

'Our remaining ancient woodland covers less than 2% of the UK, and is irreplaceable.'

CRYPTIC CREATURES, PUZZLING PLANTS

Unravel the following:
BET
Y
Answer on page 145

IT'S IN THE BLOOD

Moles are mammals, yet they can pursue hugely active lives tunnelling away under the earth where oxygen is not so much thin on the ground, as thin in it. How do they do this? The answer lies in the blood. They have twice as much of it, and twice as much haemoglobin, as other mammals their size. In addition, the haemoglobin has a further enhanced ability when it comes to soaking up whatever oxygen it can find, turning the little creature into a virtual velvet sponge.

But moles aren't alone in this adaptation. On the other side of the world, in the high Andean mountains where oxygen is thin in the air, llamas have developed a similarly efficient internal blood system to cope with their environment.

CUTE LITTLE CRACKERS

Do you remember those porcelain animals that used to fall out of Christmas crackers or nestle at the bottom of teabag boxes? Wade Whimsies were one of the most enduring collectables of the 20th century, celebrating their 50th anniversary in 2003.

The figures – pets, British countryside animals, African wildlife and so on – were first produced by Wade Ceramics of Burslem, Stoke-on-Trent in the 1950s as miniature versions of pre-war designs, aimed at the children's market. They were so successful that 50 were produced in the 1950s, and a further 60 in the 1970s.

And they're still in production, with new designs appearing regularly. Today, collectors fall over themselves at international get-togethers to pick up the rarities, which can fetch dozens of pounds in good condition.

STRANGELY OMITTED FROM
THE I-SPY BOOK OF ANIMALS

Basilisk
Rarely seen, and when seen, rarely recorded, as has the
ability to wither the young naturalist by catching the eye,
or by breathing noxious fumes. Do not prod with stick,
as its venom can travel up the stick to your hand.
Score 25 pts. If still alive after encounter, score 50 pts.

YOU DIDN'T NEED TO KNOW THESE, BUT...

The skin of a polar bear is black
Rats cannot vomit
Porcupines float in water
If an octopus becomes excessively stressed it might eat itself
Ants stretch when they wake up
Some lions will mate over 50 times a day

SITES FOR SORE EYES

Hannah Hauxwell, who became something of a celebrity some years ago once television discovered her solitary farming life, worked her land using traditional methods only, shunning artificial fertilisers and re-seeding techniques. For over 50 years, she ran Low Birk Hat Farm in County Durham, and upon her retirement in 1988, the Durham Wildlife Trust bought the land.

Now known as Hannah's Meadow, the reserve has changed very little over the centuries. Few sites anywhere in the country are as species-rich: meadow fox tail, sweet vernal grass and crested dog's-tail mix with wild flowers such as ragged robin, marsh marigold, yellow rattle and globeflower. The Trust continues to manage the reserve by traditional methods: sheep lamb in the spring in the hay meadows; once the haycrop is cut in late July, the grass is allowed to grow until September, when it is grazed by cattle. The sheep return in November before the winter rest period, when the dry stone walls are maintained, until the cycle can begin anew.

MAN DEFINED

How to get from every creature that's ever lived
to mankind in just eight easy steps:
Kingdom: *Animalia*
Phylum: *Chordata*
Subphylum: *Vertebrata*
Class: *Mammalia*
Order: *Primates*
Family: *Hominidae*
Genus: *Homo*
Species: *sapiens*
Subspecies: *sapiens sapiens*

BROCK STARS

How to find out if there's a badger sett in your vicinity. If you do find one, however… don't badger it.

- Badger setts tend to be D-shaped, larger than fox-holes, and with little, if any food outside the entrance.
- Steam rising from the sett on cold winter days.
- Badger foot-prints can often be smudged, as the animal tends to put its hind paw on the same spot as the fore paw.
- Badgers are notoriously clean creatures, so look out for piles of old plant bedding, latrines and small bones. A sett is likely to be nearby.
- Scratch marks on nearby trees or posts.
- Reasonably obvious pathways, as badgers follow set routes every night.
- Round, shallow snuffle-holes, where the badgers have been searching for worms.
- Torn-up wasp nests.
- Badger hair on barbed wire fences. The hair is black and white, about 10cm long, and rough to the touch.

A CROW BY ANY OTHER NAME

Country names for the hooded crow:
Cawdy mawdy
Denman
Dunbilly
Harry Dutchman
Isle of Wight crow
Kentishman
Market Jew crow
Royston Dick

NAVIGATIONAL SYSTEMS FOR MICE

How do mice, as they scurry about at night, know whether or not they're exploring new areas, or simply scurrying round and round the same spot. According to some recent research, they could be using their own landmarks.

Researchers discovered that when wood mice came across an item that differed from most others in an environment – such as, in one experiment, a plastic white disc – it would drag it to the area where it was foraging, then scamper off. After a while, it would return to the disc, then run off in a different direction. It appeared to be using the disc as a landmark to focus its energies more efficiently. Yet plastic white discs are not all that common in the wild, so mice have to make their own landmarks. One common approach is to drag a number of leaves into a small yet distinct pile.

MEANWHILE, IN A FOREIGN LAND...

When news spread a few years ago that the tiny town of Talkeetna in Alaska hosts an annual moose dropping festival, animal activists began to sweat. This, surely, was worse even than bear-baiting and cock-fighting.

Not so. The festival celebrates not the chucking of moose off a cliff, but the animals' droppings themselves. They're thrown from a balloon, the closest to a target winning prizes. This event takes place during the second week of every July, after which the inch-long brown pellets are shellacked and sold in vast quantities to curious tourists, who snap up the turds and take them home as novelty earrings, Christmas decorations, necklaces and swizzle sticks. Cocktail, anyone?

The animals and plants of Aesop's Fables help us learn to take the rough with the smooth.

The Rose and the Amaranth
A Rose and an Amaranth blossomed side by side in a garden, and the Amaranth said to her neighbour, 'How I envy you your beauty and your sweet scent! No wonder you are such a universal favourite.' But the Rose replied with a shade of sadness in her voice, 'Ah, my dear friend, I bloom but for a time: my petals soon wither and fall, and then I die. But your flowers never fade, even if they are cut; for they are everlasting.'
Greatness carries its own penalties.

The Raven and the Swan
A Raven saw a Swan and desired to secure for himself the same beautiful plumage. Supposing that the Swan's splendid white colour arose from his washing in the water in which he swam, the Raven left the altars in the neighbourhood where he picked up his living, and took up residence in the lakes and pools. But cleansing his feathers as often as he would, he could not change their colour, while through want of food he perished.
Change of habit cannot alter nature.

The Fox and the Bramble
A Fox was mounting a hedge when he lost his footing and caught hold of a Bramble to save himself. Having pricked and grievously torn the soles of his feet, he accused the Bramble because, when he had fled to her for assistance, she had used him worse than the hedge itself. The Bramble, interrupting him, said, 'But you really must have been out of your senses to fasten yourself on me, who am myself always accustomed to fasten upon others.'
To the selfish, all are selfish

The Ant and the Grasshopper

In a field one summer's day, a Grasshopper was hopping about, chirping and singing to its heart's content. An Ant passed by, bearing along with great toil an ear of corn he was taking to the nest. 'Why not come and chat with me,' said the Grasshopper, 'instead of toiling and moiling in that way?' 'I am helping to lay up food for the winter,' said the Ant, 'and recommend you to do the same.' 'Why bother about winter?' said the Grasshopper; 'we have got plenty of food at present.' But the Ant went on its way and continued its toil. When the winter came, the Grasshopper had no food and found itself dying of hunger, while it saw the Ants distributing every day corn and grain from the stores they had collected in the summer.

It is best to prepare for the days of necessity.

THREE MEN AND A BOOK

Kenneth Grahame, a Scottish secretary to the Bank of England, was fond of telling stories about a character called Toad to his son, Alastair, who was born in 1900. Alastair was fond of hearing them, too; so much so that Grahame decided to get the tales published and try them out on a wider market. *The Wind in the Willows* was published in 1908, although initially only to a lukewarm reception. As the years went by, its popularity slowly grew, however, and AA Milne and EH Shepherd, writer and illustrator of the tales of *Winnie the Pooh*, became interested. Shepherd illustrated the book, and Milne dramatised it for the stage as *Toad of Toad Hall*.

Unlike Milne's own son Christopher Robin, however, Alastair Grahame was not to live to see the great success that his childhood tales spawned. He was killed in the Great War.

CATERWAULING

A list of feline chart-toppers:
Tiger Feet – Mud
The Cat Crept In – Mud again
The Lion Sleeps Tonight – Many, many artists
What's New Pussycat? – Tom Jones
Cool for Cats – Squeeze
Eye of the Tiger – Survivor
Three Lions (Football's Coming Home) – Lightning Seeds
Everybody wants to be a Cat – Phil Harris and
Scatman Crothers (The Aristocats)
Feline Groovy – Simon and Garfunkel
Anything by Atomic Kitten, Cat Stevens, Eartha Kitt
or Lionel Ritchie.

SITES FOR SORE EYES

It may not have the most prepossessing name, but the
ECOS Millennium Environmental Centre is the centrepiece of one of Northern Ireland's finest nature reserves.
Situated in Ballymena, Co Antrim, and run by the Ulster
Wildlife Trust with Ballymena Borough Council, the
reserve is grazed by rare Irish breeds of sheep
and cattle, keeping the organically run meadows and
grasslands perfect for breeding waders, skylarks and other
ground-nesting birds. Sedge and grasshopper warblers
breed on the reserve, while little grebe, teal and goldeneye
are among the attractions of the lake during winter. The
grasslands cover a wide spectrum of neutral and acid
swards from dry, through peaty, to various states of
dampness and periodic inundation.
The environmental centre itself provides information on
how best to manage sites for the benefit of wildlife, as
well as hints and ideas for sustainable living. You can even
hire electrically charged bikes to get around.

The swift, one of our short-staying summer visitors, is the most aerial of birds. It feeds, sleeps, drinks and even mates on the wing, alighting only to build its nest, incubate the eggs and feed its young. The mating occurs high up, for they need a long way to fall during the process. The female flies in front of the male in a horizontal flight, and he lands on top of her with his own wings held high. They move their tails back and forth in an attempt to mate, while dropping steadily. This is one of nature's only mating procedures that, should it last too long, could end in death.

This is compounded by the fact that swifts are incapable of slow flight. Their lengthy carpus bones account for their very long primary feathers. These are the feathers that produce a downward and forward thrusting force, helpful for speed, but not so useful for manoeuvrability and subtler flight.

Yet manoeuvrability is not so necessary when you barely come lower than rooftop level. Most things at that height and above tend not to move suddenly – apart from other birds. Swifts have been recorded at surprisingly old ages for such small birds, up to 21 in fact, and one of the oldest found had been killed in a collision... with another swift.

DON'T COUNT YOUR FROGS
BEFORE THEY'RE HATCHED

A frog's egg is a vulnerable thing to be. A spawning female lays around 2000 of them, yet only about 2% of them, at best, survive into adulthood.

A NATION OF INSECTS

Below are the 27 orders of British insect. The numbers in brackets are the total British species, sometimes approximated. These numbers frequently change as new classification discoveries are made.

Diptera – Two-winged flies (6670)
Hymenoptera – Bees, wasps, ants and allies (6500)
Coleoptera – Beetles (4000)
Lepidoptera – Butterflies and moths (2500)
Hemiptera – True bugs (1650)
Mallophaga – Biting lice (500)
Collembola – Springtails (300)
Trichoptera – Caddis-flies (190)
Thysanoptera – Thrips (150)
Psocoptera – Booklice (90)
Neuroptera – Lacewings (69)
Siphaptera – Fleas (60)
Anoplura – Sucking lice (50)
Ephemeroptera – Mayflies (47)
Odonata – Dragonflies and damselflies (40)
Plecoptera – Stoneflies (34)
Orghoptera – Grasshoppers and crickets (30)
Strepsiptera – Stylopids (20)
Diplura – Two-pronged bristletails (12)
Protura – Tiny wingless insects with no common name (12)
Thysanura – Bristletails (9)
Dictyoptera – Cockroaches (6)
Dermaptera – Earwigs (4)
Mecoptera – Scorpion-flies (4)
Phasmida – Stick insects (4 introduced species)
Raphidioptera – Snakeflies (4)
Megaloptera – Alderflies (3)

SNAKES ALIVE!

Britain has six species of native reptile: adder, grass snake, smooth snake, slow worm, common lizard and sand lizard. What makes them reptiles?

1. Their bodies are covered with scales or horny plates.
2. They are cold blooded, which means they control their body temperature by getting their heat directly from the sun or other warm objects, rather than from the food they eat.
3. Snakes and lizards have teeth that are continually replaced throughout their life.
4. Reptiles also shed their skins at least once a year, depending on species, and you may find a discarded, colourless skin in summer months. Shedding, or 'sloughing', allows the reptile to grow, and helps dispose of parasites, dirt and deposits on the skin.
5. The adder and the common lizard give birth to live young, but other reptiles lay eggs.
6. Please note that Jeffrey Archer is, in fact, a mammal.

THE BRITISH MONGOOSE?

Probably the only British mammal to make a habit of killing and eating adders is the hedgehog, which not only carries a certain immunity to the snake's venom, but also carries at least 6000 other weapons – its spikes. By poking and prodding at the adder, slipping in little bites when it can, the hedgehog lures the snake into an attack, which it fends off with its spikes. Impaling or wounding itself on the sharp points, the snake steadily weakens, until it is incapable of further attacks or flight. Then the hedgehog pounces, and the battle is over.

CATCH THE MOUSE

The black dots are mice running around a maze.
To catch one, all you have to do is stare at it.

SHELLING OUT

The seven species of marine turtle around the world are:
Australian flatback
Olive Ridley
Loggerhead
Kemp's Ridley
Green
Hawksbill
Leatherback
All but the first two have been recorded in British and
Irish waters. The first specific identification was of
a leatherback in 1756 off Cornwall. It ended up
as a centrepiece in a Penzance feast.

108

SITES FOR SORE EYES

Monkwood, near Worcestershire's Sinton Green, has a long and deserved reputation as a magnificent reserve for butterflies and moths. 36 species of the former have been seen here, along with over 500 species of moth. Wood white, white admiral and silver-washed fritillary are among the highlights, but look out too for dragonfly specialities such as the emperor.

If butterflies are in abundance, then the reserve must boast an impressive floral variety, and it does. Spring brings early purple orchids, lily-of-the-valley, ragged robin and ramsons. Knapweed, meadowsweet, melilot and betony are among the summer attractions, while autumn introduces an impressive display of fungi. The reserve is jointly owned by the Worcestershire Wildlife Trust and Butterfly Conservation.

A BUNCH OF DICKY BIRDS

Frog and toad – road
Apples and pears – stairs
Pig's ear – beer
Rabbit and pork – talk
Daisy roots – boots
Hearts of oak – broke
Flounder and dab – cab
Grasshopper – copper
Turtle dove – love
Haddock and bloater – motor (car)
Salmon and trout – pint of stout
Tom tit – Nobody knows what this is supposed to mean, but it may be some kind of faecal product

Peat is an organic material that forms in the water-logged, sterile, acidic conditions of bogs and fens. These conditions favour the growth of mosses, especially sphagnum. As plants die, they do not decompose. Instead, the organic matter is laid down, and slowly accumulates as peat because of the lack of oxygen in the bog.

A little over 3% of the earth's land surface is covered in peat, but not all peatlands are the same. Just as forests in Brazil, Canada and England are very different, so too are peatlands in Alaska, Indonesia and Europe, each supporting its own native plants and animals. Peat has the ability to preserve materials and this has led to some remarkable finds in peat bogs, including people buried thousands of years ago and wooden artefacts that have not survived elsewhere.

The importance of peatlands has been recognised by the European Union, which has identified a number of bogs as priority habitats for conservation under the Habitats and Species Directive. Peat bogs contribute to the welfare of all living things by 'locking up' carbon that would otherwise increase the greenhouse effect. Carbon, removed from the atmosphere over thousands of years, is released when bogs are drained and peat starts to decompose.

Originally, lowland raised bog (the rarest type in the UK) covered nearly 95,000ha. Now only 6000ha remain in a near natural state.

Agriculture and forestry have damaged large areas of peatland. But today, commercial peat extraction to supply gardeners and nursery growers is the major threat. Peat has been cut and used as a fuel for many centuries. Hand-cutting of peat is a slow, labour-intensive process that can allow the bog partially to recover. It is very different from industrialised, mechanical extraction practised by peat companies, which drain and damage whole bogs. The companies deep-drain peatlands and strip all vegetation from vast expanses of bog surface.

Peat bogs desperately need your help. You can help save them by:

• Refusing to buy peat or plants grown in peat. If your garden centre doesn't stock them, ask why not. Details of where to buy peat-free products are available from The Wildlife Trusts.

• Stop using peat in your garden; start a compost heap that will provide an alternative.

• Find out if your local authority has signed the peatland protection charter (details from your local Wildlife Trust).

• Visit a peatland reserve near to you and see its wildlife. (Your local Wildlife Trust can help you.) Once you have, you'll never want to buy peat again.

FROGS ARE FUNNY

A man goes into a cinema with his frog to watch a film. There's a funny scene early on, and the frog starts laughing. A little later on, the mood turns sadder and suddenly the frog starts crying.
This goes on throughout the entire film, the frog laughing and crying at all the right places. A woman nearby has been watching the whole thing and on the way out goes up to the man and says, 'That's truly amazing!'
'It certainly is,' he replies. 'He hated the book!'

HAUNTED GARDENS

The Botanic Gardens in Ventnor, on the Isle of Wight, are built on the site of a former Royal National Hospital for Chest Diseases, and patients who suffered a lingering and debilitating death from tuberculosis are believed to haunt the site.

When workmen started to demolish the hospital to build the garden in 1969, they experienced some unexplained and spine-chilling events. Firstly, all their machinery failed (they were forced to tackle the operating theatre with sledgehammers), and then they claimed to be haunted by the ghost of a consumptive young girl who watched them as they worked. Subsequent visitors also claimed to hear sounds of weeping and moaning, and a ghostly nurse has been sighted doing her rounds in the gardens. As for the slight hint of cinnamon, which pervades the site of the old outside wards (now the potting sheds), this has been linked to the patients' Christmas cinnamon punch. If you're lucky (or unlucky – whichever way you want to look at it), you may be one of the few who see the hospital building itself appear, rising in a shattered mist out of the ghostly beauty of the garden.

NINE PLANTS THAT THINK THEY'RE ANIMALS

Clianthus puniceus	Parrot's bill
Ilex ferox	Hedgehog holly
Hedera helix	Dragon's claw ivy
Acanthus mollis	Bear's breeches
Stachys byzantina	Lamb's ears/Bunnies' ears
Chenopodium album	Lamb's quarters/Fat hen
Acalypha hispida	Monkey tail
Heliconia rostrata	Lobster claws
Silene pendula	Nodding catchfly

Bald as a coot
Their white head patches give coots an appearance of baldness.

As happy as a clam at high tide
At high tide, clams are free from the attentions of their predators.

The bee's knees
Bees carry pollen back to the hive in sacs on their legs. The allusion is to the concentrated goodness to be found around the bee's knee.

Crocodile tears
Crocodiles have glands that secrete liquid to keep their eyelids moist when out of the water. These glands are sometimes stimulated when the crocodile is eating.

Pop goes the weasel
To pop is to pawn something, and a weasel and stoat is a coat. Thus, once you've been in and out of the eagle (a pub), you've run out of money and have to pawn your clothes. Well, that's the way the money goes.

Raining cats and dogs
The phrase is supposed to have originated in the 17th century. City streets were filthy and heavy rain would often carry along dead animals. Richard Brome's *The City Witt*, 1652, includes the line: 'It shall rain dogs and polecats'.

Weasel words
Words that suck the life out of the words next to them, just as a weasel sucks the egg and leaves the shell.

White elephant
White, or albino, elephants were regarded as holy in ancient Thailand: to keep one was a very expensive task. Thus, a gift of a white elephant was an unwanted thing, for it would ruin you.

Make the beast with two backs
An older phrase than might be assumed. In *Othello*, Iago explains: 'I am one, sir, that comes to tell you your daughter and the Moor are now making the beast with two backs'.

POTTERING AROUND THE CEMETERY

Beatrix Potter, whose books have been stored in the child-hood nostalgia banks of a century's worth of readers, created a range of countryside characters whose names are known to many. But where did those names come from: a fertile imagination?

The answer appears to be a little more morbid. Potter was born in London at 2 Bolton Gardens, West Brompton, just up the road from Brompton Cemetery, where she probably often took youthful strolls.
Many of the headstones have disappeared over the years, swallowed up by lengthening grasses, the names they bore worn away by the decades. Yet recent research has revealed that some of the inhabitants of the cemetery bore a surprising resemblance to Potter's characters.

William McGregor and Kelvin Brock alone could have been put down to coincidence – Farmer McGregor and Tommy Brock (from The Tailor of Gloucester) aren't particularly unusual names – but by the time you get to Noel Nutkins (Squirrel Nutkin?), eyebrows are beginning to rise. Further down the list you come to Jeremiah Fisher (Jeremy Fisher?), and you know you're on to something. If only there was a clincher...

And there is. In addition to those above, Brompton grave-yard was also the final resting place of one Peter Rabbett.

CRYPTIC CREATURES, PUZZLING PLANTS

My goodness, what connects the following:
Ostrich; toucan; kangaroo; bear; seal; pelican; tortoise; lion; kinkajou?
Answer on page 145

RESEARCH ALL WASHED UP

In 2001 researchers from Bristol University were amazed to find that bats they were monitoring with radio transmitters had all taken to the water. Bats often fly low over water, taking insects with their feet, and should they accidentally find themselves in the water, can get out... but this was different. The signals received from the transmitters showed one bat slowly moving into a pool of water, gradually joined by the others, until they had crossed to the other side. The researchers were dumbfounded and excited. Was this new behaviour being exhibited?

Meanwhile, another group of researchers from Oxford University had been monitoring voles. They too reported on some extra ordinary mammalian behaviour. Also using radio transmitters, they observed the voles launch themselves into the air... and stay there, reaching speeds of up to six miles per hour as they twisted and turned in the night sky. *Voler* may be French for 'to fly', but this was ridiculous.

Some time later, the two groups happened to meet up. Each told the other of their fascinating findings. Each mentioned the night they'd been researching: it was the same one. Each revealed the stretch of water they'd been monitoring: it was the same one.

Each began slowly to realise that they'd been using identical radio frequencies, and monitoring each other's animals.

A WORLD IN MICROCOSM

There are more organisms in a spadeful of soil than there are humans on the planet.

OH NO! IT'S THEM!

There are about 50 different species of ant in Britain, many of which are impossible to tell apart without the aid of a good microscope. But the ants themselves know the differences, and in some cases, exploit them. The magnificently titled blood-red slave-making ant is not a species you want living near you if you're, say, a wood ant, for the slave-makers live up to their name.

In around July or August, they make their raids. A party of workers sets out early in the morning until they find the nest of another species, which they then encircle. Once their numbers are high enough, they enter the nest and grab as many of the pupae inside that they can find. It's a desperate affair. Workers from the invaded nest are killed if they attack, while the other ants try to break through the invading lines with their pupae, or carry them away by climbing up vegetation. They are rarely successful.

Returning to their own nest with the pupae clamped in their jaws, the slave-makers have finished their job. The pupae will hatch and become workers themselves in their new colony.

A TOAD BY ANY OTHER NAME

Country names for the common toad
Bulgranack
Gangril
Hornywink
Jack
Josey
Puddock
Slug
Winky

IDENTITY CRISIS

People who might be surprised to find that they're
actually creatures or plants:

Cherry Laurel is a shrub
Douglas Fir is a tree
Herb Robert is a flower
Holly Blue is a butterfly
Jack Snipe is a bird
John Dory is a fish
Matt Knight is a fungus
Rose Chafer is a beetle
Phil Tufnell is a rabbit

YOU'RE SURE OF A BIG SURPRISE

When a home-owner in Henley-on-Thames called in the
police to investigate a break-in in 2002, she was worried
that her basement might have been burgled. Nothing
seemed to have been stolen, however, and the DNA testing
on some blood found by the broken window revealed that
if anything had been stolen, it couldn't have been anything
larger than could fit in a wallaby's pouch. It seemed that the
animal must have fallen into her basement area, broken
the window, pulled itself together, and with one bound
was free.

Wallabies are probably the most unusual of wild British
animals. Escapes from parks and collections, generally in
the south or the Midlands, they are not particularly
successful, but the occasional colony survives for a while.
In 1993, the estimated feral population in Britain was just
30, although this may have fallen in more recent years.

SPOT THE DOG

He's in there somewhere.

A NEW FLAVOUR IN HOSPITAL FOOD?

Garlic has long been known to keep Dracula at bay. Now,
the miracle-worker has turned its attention to another
creature that steals lives at night and is invisible by day.
'Hospital superbugs', as they've been dubbed, have
become the scourges of today's medicine, mainly
by infecting surgical wounds. MRSA (methicillin-resistant
Staphylococcus aureus) kills up to 2000 patients per year
in Britain alone, and antibiotics have so far proved of little
value in combating its strength.
Enter the garlic plant. Used in medicine for centuries, the
plant contains allicin, which has been discovered to be
capable of killing MRSA and many other 'superbugs'.
Another case of traditional medicines being the best?

SITES FOR SORE EYES

The mighty Chobham Common, run by the Surrey Wildlife Trust, is a true delight for lovers of heathland wildlife. Covered with sweeps of purple heather, amongst which is an array of mini-habitats, there's plenty to see.

No fewer than 26 species of mammal live here – including the water vole – as do grass snakes, common and sand lizards. The site is also of UK importance for spiders, ladybirds, bees and wasps: keep an eye open, too, for Dartford warbler and hobby. The reserve is rich in history. Its patchwork of habitats was first created by prehistoric farmers 6000 years ago, while the common was given to the Abbot of Chertsey by sub-King Frithuwold in 676 AD. Queen Victoria herself reviewed her troops here before the Crimean War.

LEARNING FROM NATURE

Cockleburs produce small seed-bearing fruit covered with stiff, hooked spines. The spines have a purpose: by attaching themselves to fur or clothing, they are carried far and wide, distributing the plant around the world.

In 1948, amateur Swiss naturalist George de Mestral returned from a walk covered in burrs and, in a fit of curiosity, examined them. Looking at the burrs under a microscope, he noticed each one consisted of hundreds of tiny hooks that 'grabbed' onto loops of thread or fur. Inspired by their design, and realising that this hook and loop method could work equally well with clothing, he invented Velcro, short for 'velour crochet', or 'crocheted velvet'.

WATER SPREAD

Canadian waterweed is the best known example of an alien aquatic plant 'rooting' itself in Britain, but it is not alone, as this list of introduced species with their first recorded dates shows:

Sweet-flag..1668
Canadian waterweed...1842
Bog arum..1861
Tapegrass..1868
Grass-leaved naiad...1883
Water fern...1886
Cape-pondweed..1906
Canadian arrowhead..1908
Duck-potato...1941
Various-leaved water-milfoil..1941
Curly waterweed...1944
Red water-milfoil..1944
South American waterweed...1948
Large-flowered waterweed..1953
New Zealand pigmyweed...1956
Parrot's-feather..1960
Narrow-leaved arrowhead...1962
Spatter-dock..1963
Nuttall's waterweed...1966
Fanwort..1969
Least duckweed...1977
Slender sweet-flag...1986
Floating pennywort..1990

YOU'RE SURE OF A BIG SURPRISE

If you thought the only sizeable item on Salisbury Plain
was Stonehenge, then it may be time to rethink. In
November 2003, permission was given to reintroduce
the great bustard to the area, a bird that was hunted to
extinction in Britain in the 19th century. For 10 years
from June 2004, 40 chicks will be introduced to the area
each year from abandoned nests in Russia. If all goes well
these will grow into huge whiskered turkey-like birds,
each the size of an adult roe deer.

A similar programme at Porton Down was tried but
failed in the 70s, yet hopes are high that the Salisbury
Plain experiment will work, particularly in Wiltshire itself,
for the bird adorns the county's coat of arms. The Porton
Down birds were bred in captivity, but by releasing these
new birds straight into the wild, it is believed that they
will be better able to fend for themselves.

CRYPTIC CREATURES, PUZZLING PLANTS

Which of the following is not a moth?
Transparent burnet
Great burnet
Five-spot burnet
Six-spot burnet
New Forest burnet
Answer on page 145

MEANWHILE, IN A FOREIGN LAND

An 80-year-old elephant in Thailand was given a new
lease of life in 2003. Unable to chew her food, Morakot
had become so weak that even injected saline solution,
vitamins and antibiotics seemed unlikely to save her life.
So another solution was found: dentures. These were
made from stainless steel, silicone and plastic,
and measured six inches in width and length.

Elephants normally grow four sets of teeth during
a lifetime, but once they've lost their last molar they
cannot chew properly and often die from malnutrition
or starvation. Unless, of course, there's a handy
elephant dentist nearby.

ANIMAL CRACKERS

Zoos around the world have been going through difficult
times in recent years. Many have had to reshape their
function, concentrating on education, conservation issues,
and protection of endangered species to encourage people
worried about seeing animals in captivity back through the
turnstiles. Yet one zoo in Dandong, China, recently tried
a rather novel approach to its marketing strategy. It
handed out rifles at the gate and allowed its visitors to
shoot the animals.

Protests naturally rang out, but the zoo defended itself
by stating that the animals were being shot under
controlled circumstances, it was only a bit of fun, and,
anyway, folks weren't allowed to shoot the rare ones, good
heavens no.

It seems that such a carefully constructed argument fell
on deaf ears, and the zoo reverted to the old-fashioned
approach of animal protection in 2003.

A TURNER FOR THE BOOKS

William Turner (1508-68) has been dubbed the Father
of British Botany for his extensive cataloguing of British
flora. He was the first to publish the names of several
plants. Among today's rarities to be first recorded
by Turner are:

Corncockle
Dittander
Pasqueflower
Pheasant's eye
Thorow-wax
Wild cabbage
Wild pear

SMELL A RAT?

One of the greatest mammalian success stories is that of the
brown rat. By the year 1700, the animal was not found west
of the Volga, but some believe that an Asian earthquake
helped to get its population moving. Within a short time,
it had made first Russia, then Europe its own, reaching:

- Denmark in 1716
- Britain in 1720 (probably on a Russian timber ship)
- Ireland in 1722
- France in 1750
- Norway in 1762 (although their Latin name is
Rattus norvegicus, they did not reach this land until
comparatively late)
- Spain and Italy in the early 19th century.

In 1777, the natural historian Gilbert White noted that the
black rat was already being steadily replaced by the
'Norwegian' newcomer.

Some plants beginning with B in the works of Shakespeare:

Captain: 'Tis thought the king is dead; we will not stay. The BAY trees in our country are all wither'd, And meteors fright the fixed stars of heaven.
Richard II, Act 2, Scene 4

Maria: Get ye all three into the BOX-tree: Malvolio's coming down this walk: he has been yonder i' the sun practising behaviour to his own shadow this half hour: observe him, for the love of mockery; for I know this letter will make a contemplative idiot of him.
Twelfth Night, Act 2, Scene 5

Cordelia: Alack, 'tis he: why, he was met even now As mad as the vex'd sea; singing aloud; Crown'd with rank fumiter and furrowweeds, With BURDOCKS, hemlock, nettles, cuckoo-flowers, Darnel, and all the idle weeds that grow In our sustaining corn.
King Lear, Act 4, Scene 4

Duke Vincentio: We have strict statutes and most biting laws... Now, as fond fathers, Having bound up the threatening twigs of BIRCH, Only to stick it in their children's sight For terror, not to use, in time the rod Becomes more mock'd than fear'd; so our decrees, Dead to infliction, to themselves are dead; And liberty plucks justice by the nose; The baby beats the nurse, and quite athwart Goes all decorum.
Measure for Measure, Act 1, Scene 3

Second Carrier: Peas and BEANS are as dank here as a dog, and that is the next way to give poor jades the bots: this house is turned upside down since Robin Ostler died.
King Henry IV, Part 1, Act 2, Scene 1

Flute: Most radiant Pyramus, most lily-white of hue, Of colour like the red rose on triumphant BRIER,

Most brisky juvenal and eke most lovely Jew, As true as truest horse that yet would never tire, I'll meet thee, Pyramus, at Ninny's tomb.
A Midsummer Night's Dream, Act 3, Scene 1

Pistol: Elves, list your names; silence, you airy toys. Cricket, to Windsor chimneys shalt thou leap: Where fires thou find'st unraked and hearths unswept, There pinch the maids as blue as BIL-BERRY: Our radiant queen hates sluts and sluttery.
The Merry Wives of Windsor, Act 5, Scene 5

Rosalind: There is a man haunts the forest, that abuses our young plants with carving 'Rosalind' on their barks; hangs odes upon hawthorns and elegies on BRAMBLES, all, for-sooth, deifying the name of Rosalind: if I could meet that fancy-monger I would give him some good coun-sel, for he seems to have the quotidian of love upon him.
As You Like It, Act 3, Scene 2

SITES FOR SORE EYES

Britain's wildlife isn't just land-based – some of the most fascinating sights the country has to offer are under water, and Purbeck Marine Wildlife Centre, off Dorset's Wareham coast, is a snorkeller's and rockpooler's delight.

Unusually, the reserve, run by the Dorset Wildlife Trust, has a double low tide, offering plenty of opportunity for wildlife watching. Blenny, goby, pipe-fish, squat lobster and brittlestar are among the highlights of rockpool searches, while divers can enjoy watching corkwing wrasse build their nests in the spring, or the beautiful pink sea fan at its most easterly known stronghold.

Yet if you're not too wild about submerging yourself in the water, no matter. The newly built marine centre provides you with, among many other things, superb video links to the sights and colours of the Dorset underwater coast.

NATURAL MYTHS

Mayflies live for a day only

Not true. They can live for up to a year as a developing larva; it is only in their adult, or imago, stage that life can last for just a matter of hours. The larva lives in well-oxygenated waters, feeding on microscopic plants and detritus. Among other insects, moulting generally takes place during this stage, yet not with the mayfly.

After perhaps a year of this slothlike development, life suddenly moves into fast-forward. A sub-imago emerges from the larval skin which then moults to become the full-grown adult. Males swarm to entice females towards them, then once mating has taken place, the female often drops its eggs back into the water. This has to happen quickly, as the adult mayfly is not able to feed. The eggs settle in the water or rocks, and the lengthy process with its frantic climax starts all over again.

THE BATS OF BRITAIN

Lesser horseshoe
Greater horseshoe
Whiskered
Brandt's
Natterer's
Daubenton's
Bechstein's
Common pipistrelle
Soprano pipistrelle
Nathusius' pipistrelle
Brown long-eared
Grey long-eared
Barbastelle
Serotine
Noctule
Leisler's

AN OLD ELEPHANT JOKE?

Question: How do you cure an elephant of insomnia?

*Answer: Rub into its shoulders a concoction of salt,
olive oil and water.*

If you're not laughing, that's because this isn't a joke, but
a treatment prescribed by Aristotle himself for mahouts
everywhere. The health of elephants seemed to have been
quite a preoccupation of the thinkers of the ancient
world. Solinus, for example, noted that should an
elephant eat a chameleon by mistake, then it should chew
quickly on an olive as an antidote to its poison – he
recommended that people should do the same. Aristotle
warned against excessive olive consumption for
elephants, however, particularly if they have been
topping up on their iron content.

Meanwhile – Aristotle again – if you want your elephant
to bear you boldly into war, the best way to stir up
its passions is to give it grape or rice wine to get it
fighting drunk.

PLANTS WITH A BIT OF BOUNCE
IN THEIR NAME

Spring crocus
Spring gentian
Spring snowflake
Spring squill
Spring vetch
Springbeauty

IMAGINE THESE TUNNELLING
UNDER YOUR FLOWERBEDS

The word 'mammoth' has entered the vernacular in such
a way that it's hard to believe that it could ever have
meant anything other than 'pretty darn big'. Yet the root
of the word probably comes from the Estonian
meaning 'earth-mole'.

Mammoths, whose carcasses survived the Ice Age
through preservation in permafrost, frequently turned
up through the millennia since their extinction half-
buried in the ground – indeed, Siberia still hosts some
examples. As extinct creatures were unknown,
people presumed that the mammoth still existed,
and as no one ever saw a live one, they were believed to
be subterranean creatures that, should they accidentally
tunnel to the surface, would die upon contact with the
air. In some parts of Siberia, the myth still exists today,
and newly found remains are quickly destroyed, as the
'earth-mole' is deemed to bring bad luck.

TEASEL DO

Teasel is unique in the plant world in the way in which
it blooms. Its flowers first appear in a ring around the
middle of the head, and spread slowly outwards.
As the blooms are fairly short-lived, the new growths
outlive the central growths, effectively creating two
further rings that move slowly towards the top and
bottom of the head. By the time the plant has released
all its seeds, it dies, leaving behind a tough structure
surrounded by stiff, sharp bristles. This makes it
the ideal tool for 'teasing' wool, a process practised
since Roman times.

MEANWHILE, IN A FOREIGN LAND...

The rarest parrot in the world is also the largest, and quite probably the strangest, too. New Zealand is famous for hosting the kiwi, but it's also home to the flightless kakapo, an 8lb parrot that once roamed the islands in its hundreds of thousands, but now is reduced to a few dozen individuals, thanks to its defencelessness against introduced predators, including man.

Before 1845, which was when Europeans first clapped eyes on the kakapo (known also as the owl-parrot for its nocturnal habits and facial resemblance), Maoris used the bird for meat and its feathers for cloaks, yet the population still remained fairly stable. The gold-diggers of the late 19th century lived in some cases on a diet of nothing but kakapo – rather bravely, as the bird has a strong, musky scent.

This wonderful bird possesses a haunting booming call, uttered at a low frequency and backed by occasional screeching. It also breeds on average only once every two to four years.

YOU'RE SURE OF A BIG SURPRISE

Grazing animals such as cattle and sheep are common agents of conservation in Britain... but water buffalo? These European imports have for several years been farmed in this country for their mozzarella-making milk and reduced-fat meat, but a few sites, such as The Wildlife Trust of South and West Wales' River Teifi, are now using them as part of their habitat management.

The buffalo are phenomenal grazers, and the reserve benefited not only from their reduction of invasive plants but also from the shallow dragonfly pools and wader scrapes that were the result of their wallowing. They make a remarkable sight as you come round the corner, too.

WHEN IS A GOOSE NOT A GOOSE?

For centuries, the barnacle goose was thought to be a fish. This was because the bird, which graces Europe in the winter, flies off to the Arctic to breed in the summer. As people had no idea where it went, and never saw either eggs or goslings, they assumed it must be the offspring of creatures often found near its watery habitat, ie barnacles. Believing the goose grew within large bivalves until mature, they reasoned it was a fish, thus allowing Catholics to eat it on Fridays. The belief existed in many areas until the 18th century: one species of barnacle is even named *Lepas anatifera* – 'goose-bringer' – a title bestowed by Linnaeus in 1767.

IS YOU IS OR IS YOU AIN'T MY BABY?

The cuckoo is well-known for its ability to lay an egg in another bird's nest, pull back, and watch the foster parent seemingly not notice as the adopted young pushes the other eggs and young out of the nest, continually yells for food, and grows larger than the adult that feeds it. Over 100 species in Europe have been recorded doing the cuckoo's job for it, the commonest five in Britain being the:

1. Reed warbler
2. Dunnock
3. Meadow pipit
4. Pied wagtail
5. Robin

SITES FOR SORE EYES

About a third of the world's entire breeding population of Manx shearwater breed at Skomer, the 760-acre island off Martin's Haven in Wales, near Haverfordwest. Run by the Wildlife Trust of South and West Wales, Skomer is the place to stay overnight during June and July to hear these extraordinary birds raise the roof with their cacophonous, coughing, raucous calls. Shearwaters nest in burrows, which they wriggle into on feet that were barely made for walking, yet at sea they are completely at home, arcing above the waves on long outstretched wings for decade upon decade.

Skomer is not just home to shearwaters, however. Kittiwakes, razorbills, puffins and guillemots are also on board in good numbers. Grey seals are present all year, pupping in September, while a race of bank vole is endemic to the island. Bluebells, then red campion, thrift, sea campion and heather make the isle an ever-changing palette throughout the year. The not-too-distant Skokholm Island offers similiar treats.

CRYPTIC CREATURES, PUZZLING PLANTS

Which of the following is not a moth:
Lettuce shark,
Great leopard,
Isabelline tiger,
Waved tabby,
Rusty-spotted cat?
Answer on page 145

According to Herodotus, Aesop was a slave who lived in Samos in the 6th century BC and was eventually freed by his master. He also told some great tales.

The Vixen and the Lioness

A Vixen who was taking her babies out for an airing one balmy morning, came across a Lioness, with her cub in arms. 'Why such airs, haughty dame, over one solitary cub?' sneered the Vixen. 'Look at my healthy and numerous litter here, and imagine, if you are able, how a proud mother should feel.' The Lioness gave her a squelching look, and lifting up her nose, walked away, saying calmly, 'Yes, just look at that beautiful collection. What are they? Foxes! I've only one, but remember, that one is a Lion.'

Quality is better than quantity.

The Wolf and the Crane

A Wolf who had a bone stuck in his throat hired a Crane, for a large sum, to put her head into his mouth and draw out the bone. When the Crane had extracted the bone and demanded the promised payment, the Wolf, grinning and grinding his teeth, exclaimed: 'Why, you have surely already had a sufficient recompense, in having been permitted to draw out your head in safety from the mouth and jaws of a wolf.'

In serving the wicked, expect no reward, and be thankful if you escape injury for your pains.

The Lark and Her Young Ones

A Lark had made her nest in the early spring on the young green wheat. The brood had almost grown to their full strength and attained the use of their wings and the full plumage of their feathers, when the owner of the field, looking over his ripe crop, said, 'The time has come when I must ask all my neighbours to help me with my harvest.' One of the young

Larks heard his speech and related it to his mother, inquiring of her to what place they should move for safety. 'There is no occasion to move yet, my son,' she replied; 'the man who only sends to his friends to help him with his harvest is not really in earnest.'

The owner of the field came again a few days later and saw the wheat shedding the grain from excess of ripeness. He said, 'I will come myself tomorrow with my labourers, and with as many reapers as I can hire, and will get in the harvest.' The Lark on hearing these words said to her brood, 'It is time now to be off, my little ones, for the man is in earnest this time; he no longer trusts his friends, but will reap the field himself.'

Self-help is the best help.

NATURAL MYTHS

Bread and milk is good for hedgehogs

Not true. Hedgehogs will lap it up, but they shouldn't be eating it. The bread can swell in the stomach, causing potential intestinal problems for the animal, while milk contains lactose, of which many animals are intolerant, causing diarrhoea and possibly dehydration.

Milk can also harbour bacteria for which a hedgehog has no tolerance. During summer months, hedgehogs need to drink plenty of water, but if they assuage their thirst with milk, they could suffer from dehydration. (One observer in June 1997 watched a hedgehog lapping at water continually for 75 minutes, the animal averaging three laps per second.) Finally, of course, if left outside too long on a summer night, the milk might curdle.

No, bread and milk is not good for hedgehogs.

IF YOU GO DOWN TO THE WOODS TODAY

Want to make a wooden object? Then you need the right type of wood. Traditional uses for different woods include:

Alder	Clogs and broom handles, fencing
Ash, Common	Oars, paddles, tool shafts and handles walking sticks, arrow shafts
Beech, Common	Mallets, yokes
Black Poplar	Matchsticks
Blackthorn	Walking sticks, rake teeth, chessmen
Damson	Cabinet making
Elder	Spoons
Oak	Furniture, house beams, ships
Hazel	Hurdles, basketry, crate hoops, building material
Hornbeam	Mallet heads, chopping blocks, wheel spokes
Laburnum	Cabinet making
Lime	Musical instruments, spoons
Rowan	Tool handles and carving
Scots Pine	Furniture, railway sleepers
Silver Birch	Broom bristles, tool handles
Sycamore	Furniture, musical instruments, utensils
Walnut	Furniture
White Willow	Cricket bats, trugs
Wild Cherry	Tobacco pipes
Yew	Bows

CRYPTIC CREATURES, PUZZLING PLANTS

Which of these botannical words has not been
spelt correctly?
delphinium
fuchsia
sepal
saxifrage
groundsel
Answer on page 145

LEARNING FROM NATURE

American footballers and motorbikers may one day owe their lives to woodpeckers, as the bird's extraordinary skull design is being studied to help enhance the resistance to impact of crash helmets. The woodpecker drums its beak against the bark of a tree at about 15 beats per second for a variety of reasons: alerting other woodpeckers to its territory, driving into the bark for beetles, and opening up a nest cavity in the trunk itself. If you or I had a beak and tried these tricks, we'd break our puny necks, or give ourselves brain damage at the very least.

But not the woodpecker. The bird is able to bypass the trauma thanks to a system of muscular support structures at the back of its neck, a brain cavity packed with spongy shock-absorbent bone, another cavity, also shock-absorbent, in which the tongue sits coiled up, and the ability to hammer at a completely straight angle, so that all these counter-balances align. This means that, with every single ram of their head, woodpeckers can withstand the equivalent of 250 times the gravitational force felt by astronauts as they sit in their launching rockets.

THE LIZARD'S DE-TAILS

Lizards have the ability to shed their tails for protection in a process known as 'autotomy'. The tail bones have a special weak spot at which a contraction of the muscles causes the bone to break and the tail to become loose.

The separated tail continues to wriggle for several minutes, holding the attention of the predator, and the tailless lizard can make its escape.

After some months, the lizard grows a new tail, usually stumpier than the original and less flexible. Slow worms are also capable of autotomy, but are rarely able to grow a new tail afterwards.

WOULD YOU LIKE CRAB WITH YOUR MUSSELS?

We're all used to the possibility of finding insects in our food, but few expect to find a crab lurking there. The pea crab, which has a shell under a centimetre in diameter, makes its life in bivalves, such as mussels and clams, up and down the coast. One survey of the Western Solent found that 54% of the mussels collected had pea crabs living in them. The little crab, a 'pinnotheres' species, enjoys what, to humans, is an unappetising relationship with its hosts. It lays its eggs inside the bivalves, and feeds on the mussel's mucus from around its gills. It's likely that the mussel, meanwhile, eats the crab's faeces, as they're probably swept into its gills. When the crab isn't living inside mussels, it isn't averse to a meal of faeces, either, following periwinkles around for the deposited titbits they leave behind.

MEANWHILE, IN A FOREIGN LAND...

In 1909, US President Teddy Roosevelt set off with an entourage of friends on one of the most destructive hunting safaris of all time. Starting in Mombasa, Kenya, they spent eight months blasting their way to Khartoum in Sudan. By the time they arrived, they had wiped out 5013 mammals, 4453 birds, 2322 reptiles and amphibians, plus taken a huge and uncounted number of fish, insects, shells, and plants. The remains were sent to the Smithsonian Institute, where it was found that two subspecies were among the number: Teddy had succeeded in shoving a little further towards extinction both the Roosevelt's gazelle and the Roosevelt's sable. The sable that was named after him is now one of Africa's most endangered antelope races. Talk about shooting yourself in the foot.

ANIMAL CRACKERS

Japanese TV game shows are well-known the world over for encouraging their contestants to do bizarre things with animals – eating them, letting them crawl over them, being bitten by them. Yet the stupidity crown must now surely be passed to Chilean TV, which came up with the magnificent idea of the ultimate challenge. To win a car, all 30-year-old Maria Eugenia Berrios had to do was stay in a circus cage with two lions and two tigers for three minutes. It could work. But to spice it up, she had to pat one of them on the head.

Accepting the challenge, Maria entered the cage, gingerly approached one of the tigers, and gave it a pat. Minutes later, while being rushed to hospital with serious head and leg injuries, she must have wondered how badly she'd really wanted that car. Interestingly, Chilean TV management was furious with the game show producers for their 'irresponsibility'. Stronger words come to mind.

NEW BALLS, PLEASE

What happens to the 36,000 or more tennis balls used at the annual Wimbledon championships? Some of them get turned into homes. These new homes have small holes bored into them, and are attached to poles between 75cm and 1.5m off the ground. With luck, they will become inhabited by harvest mice, who can live there in comparative safety from birds of prey and weasels, which are too big to get through the hole. Harvest mice, which weigh only as much as a 20p piece, more traditionally weave their homes out of shredded grass and reeds part of the way up tall stalks. Yet intensive farming methods have brought their habitat, and in some areas their existence, under threat.

GARDEN OF ENGLAND OR
GARDEN OF EDEN?

Hybridisation between plants is not particularly uncommon, but every now and then one turns up that catches the eye more so than most. In June 1998, a hybrid orchid was discovered, new to Britain, called *xOrchiaceras melsheimeri*. Discovered in a Kent woodland, the plant is tall with a cylindrical spike and intermediate flowers. The hoods are crimson, and have tufts of red hairs, while the spur is very small, only about 1mm long.

What makes this hybrid so memorable? It was found within a mixed population of its parent plants... the man orchid and the lady orchid.
Genesis begins anew.

SITES FOR SORE EYES

The cliffs of South Gower near Port Eynon in Wales are one of the great coastal havens of Britain. A mixture of habitats merge here, from limestone grassland and scree to maritime heath, rocky foreshore and caves to relict sand dune grassland. It's the only site anywhere in Britain where yellow whitlow grass grows, while the silky wave moth is one of its flagship species. Sea-watching can barely be matched, here, either, with rare birds recorded every year, while raven, chough and Dartford warbler feature inland.

It's an impressive feeling to stand high on the cliffs knowing that ancient life once inhabited the rocks below. A dovecote was built into the cliffs in medieval times, but the caves, which were inhabited 30,000 years ago, are some of the richest Upper Paleolithic prehistoric sites in Britain.

SOMETHING TO CROW ABOUT?

In November 2000, the *Countryside and Rights of Way Act* (CRoW) gained royal assent. This was the first major step forward in countryside protection since the *Wildlife and Countryside Act 1981*. It can be broken down into five main parts:

1. Deals with the 'right to roam'.
2. Clarifies uncertainties concerning rights of way.
3. The major wildlife section, covering Sites of Special Scientific Interest (SSSIs), enforcement of the laws pertaining to offences against wildlife, and the importance of biodiversity.
4. Requires management plans for Areas of Outstanding Natural Beauty (AONBs).
5. Various details, including local-access issues, countryside management agreements, and the registration of village greens.

HANDY PLANT NAMES TO KNOW WHEN YOU'RE IN THE MOOD FOR CUSSIN'

Bloody crane's-bill
Bastard toadflax
Devil's bit scabious
Fiddle dock
Frogbit
Hoary cress
Nipplewort
Pignut
Spotted medick
Stinking iris

TRACKING WITH A DIFFERENCE

Many aerospace radar and weapon systems are given
the names of plants or animals, including:

Blue Kestrel	Radar of the Merlin ASW helicopter
Blue Tit	Early name for Sea Spray radar
Green Willow	AI radar for single seat fighters
Mamba	Mortar location radar
Orange Poodle	Low altitude radar system
Panther	Plessey GF75 surveillance radar
Possum	Low altitude air defence radar
Red Robin	CW radar for RAF Thunderbird II
Scorpion	Blue Anchor TIR for export Bloodhound
Sea Owl	GEC Marconi thermal imager
Winkle	Passive tracking system
Yellow Tiger	Fire control radar

MEANWHILE, IN A FOREIGN LAND...

Many creatures give off an alarm call as a predator
approaches, but it can be important for the other
members of their group to know which kind of predator
it is they should be fleeing, as the vervet monkey of Africa
has worked out.

When a vervet monkey sentry sees a leopard, it gives
a loud bark, the signal to other vervets to leap into the
trees, where the leopard can't reach.

Yet what if the predator is an eagle? The treetops are the
worst place to be, so the sentry emits a coughing call,
the sign to dash to the ground and hide in a bush.

If the predator is a snake, however, then a bush may be
a foolish place to hide. A third, sharper call alerts the
other vervets to stand on their hind legs to spot the snake
for themselves and keep their distance.

LAZY, HAZY DAYS OF SUMMER

We're all familiar with the concept of hibernation, the act of sleeping through the cold months to conserve energy. Yet some animals practise aestivation, a state of torpor brought on during particularly hot and dry months.

Snails are among the creatures that aestivate. Once the air loses its humidity, some species start looking for a suitable hiding period during which to hide from the seasonal dryness, digging holes into the ground before winding down their systems. Other species, however, move upwards, climbing to the tops of plant stems, secreting mucus which dries and sticks them to the plant, while closing their shell aperture too.

RAGGING ON RAGWORT

Ragwort is becoming quite an issue in Britain. The plant, with its bright yellow petals, resembles a golden daisy (to which it is related), but its attractive appearance belies an unfortunate side-effect: it is toxic to livestock. Horses, ponies and donkeys in particular are susceptible to it, and can develop potentially fatal liver damage from eating it, even if only through seeds drifting into their hay. As a result, the British Horse Society and the government have been promoting a *Ragwort Control Bill* to prevent its spread.

Yet ragwort has its admirers, too. The caterpillar of the cinnabar moth feeds off the plant, and takes on the toxic properties itself, which it advertises to potential predators via its own warning system, a heavily marked black and yellow body. Many believe that the moth could suffer through excessive clearance of ragwort. The case is a classic example of conservation versus animal welfare.

SHOULD HAVE BEEN CHOUGHED TO BITS

In 2001, a pair of choughs – coastal crows with long, curved, tomato-red beaks – were about to be released from captivity in an attempt to get the species breeding in Cornwall for the first time in nearly 50 years. A prime site had been picked. Due to Foot and Mouth Disease, however, the programme was delayed, and in the meantime, some wild choughs flew in, nested in a different site that had not been deemed worthy, and raised four chicks. Peter Marren, one of the UK's finest commentators on conservation issues, was told when investigating the story, that the wild choughs were responding to 'appropriate management'. It was as if, although the birds had drawn up their own breeding programme, mankind still had to demonstrate some overall control. 'Could it be', Marren pondered in *British Wildlife* magazine, 'that the satisfaction of bringing back a lost animal by dint of careful planning and preparation is greater than that of merely witnessing a natural event?'

ANIMAL CRACKERS

It was late one Pennsylvania night in 2000 and the Beck family were fast asleep. They heard knocking at their front door, and wondered what was going on. Suddenly, the door was flung open, and something came running heavily up the stairs. Nervously, they tiptoed from the bedroom towards the bathroom, where the thing could be heard crashing around frantically. Closing the door on it, they called the police, while inside the bathroom could be heard the sound of something kicking on a tap. As the bath filled with water, the crashing became a splashing – the sound of breaking bottles soon joined it. When the police arrived, they cautiously opened the door.
A panicking deer was thrashing around in a bubble bath it had accidentally run for itself.

ORDER, ORDER

My house is full of animals
I don't know what to do
I think I'm going crazy –
I'm living in a zoo!
Song by Darrell Bowen and Dave Holmes

On 29 March 2000, David Amess MP stood up in the House of Commons and said: 'A few weeks ago, a scurrilous article appeared that claimed that the House of Commons was full of animals. It said that the Conservative benches are full of dinosaurs, the Labour benches full of sheep and the Liberal benches full of dead parrots. As we all know, that clearly is not the case. The only animals in the House of which I am aware are the delightful guide-dog of the [then] Secretary of State for Education and Employment, the springer spaniels that sniff round the place before our proceedings start and the mouse or rat that decided to make an appearance on the floor of the Chamber a few weeks ago.'

He was begging to move that leave be given to bring in a bill to amend the *Zoo Licensing Act 1981* so as to make it unlawful to operate a circus except with the authority of a licence.

CRYPTIC CREATURES, PUZZLING PLANTS

How many birds are sent by my true love on the 12th Day of Christmas?
Answer on page 145

DURING THE COMPILATION OF THIS BOOK, THE COMPANION TEAM...

Watched 107.4 hours of nature TV programming

Came into work with bird droppings on their clothes three times

Bought a wildlife calendar in January and lost it in March

Visited 17 nature reserves

Tried to perfect their lion impressions but came off more like a troupe of constipated baboons

Finally worked out the difference between pearl-bordered and small pearl-bordered fritillary

Mentioned the word 'fossa' 453 times

Fed 209 pigeons in the park, probably illegally

Developed a new and unexpected interest in lichens

Found the calendar again in May

Started testing the comparative strengths of crab grips. Stopped after the first one

Decided that frogs aren't particularly funny after all

Please note that although every effort has been made to ensure accuracy in this book, the above facts may be the result of wild and woolly minds.

CRYPTIC CREATURES, PUZZLING PLANTS

The answers. As if you needed them.

P6   Nightingale
P16   Beech
P21   Linnet
P26   Fox: Ox
P32   Flicker – it's an American woodpecker
P40   Eider
P42   Beagle: Eagle
P57   Zorilla – it's a striped member of the weasel family that shoots noxious anal secretions at you if you get too close
P65   Hoverfly
P93   Piddock – it's a seashore mollusc
P96   Betony
P114   They've all advertised Guinness
P121   Great burnet – it's a plant
P131   Rusty-spotted cat – it's the world's smallest species of cat, weighing just 1.5kg
P134   Botanical has only one 'n'
P143   23

WILDLIFE JOTTINGS,
IDEAS AND DOODLES

WILDLIFE JOTTINGS, IDEAS AND DOODLES

WILDLIFE JOTTINGS,
IDEAS AND DOODLES

WILDLIFE JOTTINGS,
IDEAS AND DOODLES

**WILDLIFE JOTTINGS,
IDEAS AND DOODLES**

WILDLIFE JOTTINGS, IDEAS AND DOODLES

WILDLIFE JOTTINGS, IDEAS AND DOODLES

WILDLIFE JOTTINGS,
IDEAS AND DOODLES

WILDLIFE JOTTINGS, IDEAS AND DOODLES

WILDLIFE JOTTINGS,
IDEAS AND DOODLES

**WILDLIFE JOTTINGS,
IDEAS AND DOODLES**

WILDLIFE JOTTINGS,
IDEAS AND DOODLES

WILDLIFE JOTTINGS, IDEAS AND DOODLES

WILDLIFE JOTTINGS, IDEAS AND DOODLES

PLEASE GO WILD FOR THE FOLLOWING

This book would not have been possible without the
research, ideas, and dogged support of:
Claire Ashton, Deb Bright, Rachel Cullen,
Tim and Paulette Doncaster, Katherine Lawrey,
James Marshall, Audrey McAuliffe, Nigel Millward,
Peter Tait and Geordie Torr.